MOLIÈRE
A NEW CRITICISM

Scaramouche enseignant,   Elomire estudiant.

Qualis erit? tanto docente magistro.

L. Weyen sculp

The frontispiece of 1670

See p. 32

MOLIÈRE

A NEW CRITICISM

BY

W. G. MOORE

FELLOW AND TUTOR OF
ST. JOHN'S COLLEGE

OXFORD
AT THE CLARENDON PRESS

Oxford University Press, Ely House, London W.1

GLASGOW NEW YORK TORONTO MELBOURNE WELLINGTON
CAPE TOWN SALISBURY IBADAN NAIROBI LUSAKA ADDIS ABABA
BOMBAY CALCUTTA MADRAS KARACHI LAHORE DACCA
KUALA LUMPUR HONG KONG TOKYO

FIRST EDITION 1949
REPRINTED LITHOGRAPHICALLY IN GREAT BRITAIN
FROM CORRECTED SHEETS OF THE FIRST EDITION
1953, 1956
1962 (WITH A POSTSCRIPT), 1964, 1968

PREFACE

THE occasion of the following chapters is pedestrian and professional. The twin occupations of college tutor and university lecturer, over a period of some fifteen years, have bred in me certain doubts as to the accepted categories whereby the French classics are judged. This tentative essay of a new approach is academic, since it is the product of university teaching. But that means no more than to say that the investigation rests on the scientific study of certain texts, in the attempt to read them in something like their original proportions and features. This I have found to be possible only by ruthless sacrifice of many current notions, which pass for academic apparatus and prove to be little more than legends of quite recent growth.

What emerges from this process when applied to Molière can be simply stated. The plays are comedies written and performed according to the theatrical conditions prevalent in Paris in the middle of the seventeenth century. They are the work of a man of whom we know little more than his professional activity of actor-manager. The first step towards sound criticism of Molière seems to be, therefore, the abandonment of all assumptions regarding his philosophy and his emotions, thus allowing us freedom to interpret comedies as comedies and their author as an artist. Only so may we avoid what

Acton called the greatest sin of the historian, anachronism, the transporting into the past of conceptions and categories which belong to a later age. This has been disastrously busy with Molière. The student may find in almost any text-book material concerning his 'views', which rests on the flimsiest evidence. But he may seek in vain for a dispassionate analysis of the comic art as practised in plays which are universally acknowledged as masterpieces of comedy.

One reason for this state of affairs lies in the divorce in this country between artistic and academic criticism. What schoolboys learn about classical French is worlds away from the principles of Mr. Eliot or Mr. Strachey. This is not so in France. A scholarly edition of *Tartuffe* is by an actress. The pages of this book owe more to the incisive criticism of Louis Jouvet and Jacques Arnavon than to many professors. One has the impression that the French still know how to study in order to enjoy, whereas we have forgotten the fact that comedy, of all the arts, aims at enjoyment, depends on enjoyment, and is constructed with a view to enjoyment. Let us give up talk of ulterior motives until we are more informed as to the nature and range of the enjoyment provided. The present book is concerned to achieve no more than this, by suggesting that in Molière we may find the comic art in its most vigorous and vital expression, and that this is the matter for analysis rather than imputed assumptions and doctrines. Molière was a contemporary of the Restoration. He has its mordant wit, its irony, its social satire, and its comic premisses. Far from it being impossible to bridge the gulf between Molière and Congreve, as John Palmer thought, Molière may be much nearer to Congreve than to the apostle of good sense whom we are taught to see in his plays. To speak of Molière as 'always perfectly wise and entirely reasonable' is to sacrifice the aesthetic criticism of Molière's work to an idea, and to an idea unsupported alike in Molière's life and his art.

For the new approach here suggested I can claim but little personal responsibility. The arguments and analyses to which I have subjected Molière's plays are not original. They are the outcome of professional practice, taught me by my first guide in French literature, my father, confirmed by the criticism of colleagues and pupils and even more so by the scholar from whom as an undergraduate I learned the principles of literary method, and whose latest studies are admirable explorations towards a new point of view. To Gustave Rudler indeed this book owes much, not only for the example of the probity of his scholarship but for detailed criticism and constant encouragement.

W. G. M.

OXFORD
New Year, 1949

PREFACE TO THE NEW IMPRESSION

By many readers this little work has been all too favourably received. I could perhaps wish that it had called forth less quotation and more explorations into its subject. We are still in my view a long way from understanding the true artistry of Molière. I have tried to sketch out a new approach in a final chapter, and here I would only say that, to the authorities cited in the following pages, some which have appeared since 1949 should be added so that the record may be more or less complete. I therefore add a list of these below.[1] Perhaps I may remark that since writing this book I have had the privilege of a year's teaching in a great American university. This has put me in the debt of many graduate students who have allowed me to submit the text of Molière to fresh criticism and analysis. It has also suggested to me that Molière, perhaps of all great French writers is accessible to the American student. I should be happy to think that in this small historical reassessment the New World might produce the book that will complete (and reverse where need be) the judgements of the Old.

W. G. M.

Christmas, 1960.

[1] J. Audiberti, *Molière dramaturge*, 1954.
R. Bray, *Molière homme de théâtre*, 1954.
J. Cairncross, *New Light on Molière*, 1956.
R. Fernandez, *Molière, the man seen through the plays*, 1958.
L. Emery, *Molière, Du métier à la pensée*, 1956.
R. Garapon, *La Fantaisie verbale et le comique*, 1957.
R. Jasinski, *Molière et le Misanthrope*, 1951.
G. Mongrédien, *La Vie Privée de Molière*, 1950.
            La Vie de Molière par Grimarest, 1955.
R. Robert, 'Les Commentaires de première main sur les chefs-d'œuvre de Molière' in *Revue des Sciences Humaines*, 1956.
D. Romano, *Essai sur le comique de Molière*, 1950.
J. D. Hubert, *Molière and the Comedy of Intellect*, 1962.
J. Guicharnaud, *Molière, une aventure théâtrale*, 1963.

CONTENTS

I. RESEARCH[1]

A LEADING French scholar of America has a spirited page describing how university teachers of literature are usually thought of as obsessed by the nightmare of finding ever more subjects of research in an already well-worn field. In the eyes of an outsider, he writes, 'nous délivrerions gravement des parchemins fallacieux, tandis que la peau de chagrin qu'est l'histoire de la littérature s'est rétrécie misérablement entre nos doigts'. Yet the opposite is the truth, continues M. Peyre.[2] The good subjects abound: the best have hardly been touched, but they are too rich and complex for beginners: 'Les études de détail sont légion, mais les études d'ensemble, les synthèses exactes et pourtant compréhensives, mûries et impartiales, c'est-à-dire sachant ne point être thèses et ne point vouloir à tout prix dire ce que nul autre auparavant n'a dit, manquent encore dans bien des cas.' The words might stand as epigraph to a bibliography of Molière. Despite an imposing array of titles,[3] the accurate study of

---

[1] The substance of this chapter appeared in *French Studies*, i. 4.

[2] H. Peyre, *L'Influence des littératures antiques sur la littérature française moderne*, Yale, 1941, pp. 1–2.

[3] Saintonge and Christ, *Fifty Years of Molière Studies*, Johns Hopkins, 1942. Complete and careful, but exasperating in method. Omits A. E. Freeman's articles on 'Molière as a Reformer' in *MHRA Bulletin*, March and June 1928. Additions in *Modern Language Notes*, April 1944.

detail has yet to be accomplished in some parts of the field; the ripe, synthetic study is wanting in almost all. Yet the 'tempo' of Molière research seems to have slowed up markedly in recent years. The 'peau de chagrin' would seem to have shrivelled so rapidly that advanced students now select more 'modern' subjects. Yet the great subjects lie here still unquarried. We are still ignorant (or we still differ) as to the real nature of Molière's genius, as to the world of thought in which he moved, as to the type and quality of his mind, and as to the bases and implications of his art. One has only to look into school editions and into general works of literature to see in what contradictions even the well-informed may be involved. It is over forty years since Faguet demonstrated from the plays that Molière was a man of the most ordinary ideas, and the attitude is still common even among those who continue to speak of the dramatist as a genius. For at least one living French man of letters Molière's view of the world is as impious as Bossuet thought it was. Yet it is difficult nowadays to see French classical drama in the light in which Bossuet (excusably) saw it.[1] It is apparently still possible to regard Molière as a master of comedy and yet to think that his masterpieces are almost more tragic than comic.

What then has research in Molière been concerned with, if not the elucidation of these central problems? There are two answers to this question. The first is biography, in which an incredible mass of verbiage and calumny has been sifted, with considerable profit. Secondly, the moral and satiric aspects of the plays have been endlessly, and not so profitably, discussed. If any one point more than another can be picked on as marking a change of direction in Molière studies it is the realization, in most work done over the last twenty years, that Molière's views, the nature of his satire, his 'intention'—all such themes are dependent upon a prior determination as to the nature of his comedy. There has been a growing conviction that until we know the dramatic necessities we cannot begin to dis-

[1] F. Mauriac, *Trois grands hommes devant Dieu*, 1930.

cuss any personal views; in other words, that the plays were constructed as dramatic entertainment and not as pamphlets. To identify the author with the most reasonable person in his play is, we are coming to realize, a risky and profitless assumption. We should think of Molière, not as pillorying Alceste and therefore sharing the views of Philinte, but as imagining both elements in his contrasted pairs of characters, as the creator of Tartuffe *and* Orgon, of Arnolphe *and* Agnès.[1]

The history of the gradual infusion of scientific method into the investigation of Molière's career is a fascinating one. It has met with endless opposition. From the start, that is from the moment that he became remarked by any large number of his contemporaries, he has been misrepresented. The phenomenon is common in French literature. As there was a quarrel of *Le Cid* and of *Phèdre*, so there were quarrels over *L'École des Femmes* and *Tartuffe*. In all these cases, as in the lawsuits provoked by *Madame Bovary* and *Les Fleurs du Mal*, professional jealousy played a large, and perhaps decisive, part. The contemporary documents are meagre and have had to be laboriously disentangled from the legend around them. The first written 'Life', dating from 1728, has been shown to be hardly worth the name of source.[2] The majority of contemporary accounts are libellous. Light was brought into this jungle by the patient work of Livet, Fourier, and others in *Le Moliériste* and by industrious foreign scholars.[3] The work of fifty years was crowned (as only right) by a professor of the Sorbonne, who in three remarkable volumes exposed untrustworthy evidence and fantastic conjecture.[4] It is

[1] Cf. D. Mornet, *Histoire de la littérature française classique*, 1942, p. 269: 'La question [si Molière est Alceste ou Philinte] est peut-être oiseuse, car, lorsqu'il les imagine, il est Alceste et Philinte et Arnolphe et don Juan et Agnès et Célimène; ou même Harpagon, Tartuffe et Philaminte. Il vit leur vie. . . .'

[2] A. Tilley, 'Grimarest's Life of Molière', *Mod. Lang. Rev.* xiii (1918), pp. 439–54.

[3] e.g. K. Mantzius, *Molière*, 1908.

[4] G. Michaut, *La Jeunesse de Molière*, Hachette, 1922; *Les Débuts de Molière à Paris*, 1923; *Les Luttes de Molière*, 1925.

astonishing that we had to wait till 1920 for it to be demonstrated that Harpagon should not be taken as a portrait of Molière's father, nor Alceste as modelled on any single contemporary figure. How difficult it was to bring sober investigation into this field of study is shown by the longevity of the calumny about Molière's wife. It has been stated in countless 'lives' that he married the daughter of his mistress. The discovery of a baptismal certificate actually stating the contrary, that Armande was the younger sister of Madeleine, did not settle the question; the old view appears as fact in a recent critical study.[1]

Michaut's work has established certain positions in Molière scholarship which may by now (after an interval of over twenty years) be safely regarded as 'acquis'. It has destroyed the legend of a melancholic and subjective poet, who dramatized his own domestic troubles. In other words, the plays have been freed from the accretions of those who used them as subjective evidence. We do not now search the plays for the 'sens caché' which will reveal Molière's personal history. As Michaut says, this unscientific confusion between the works and the life had reached fantastic proportions: 'Le lecteur finit par ne plus bien savoir si c'est la tragédie supposée de son existence qui nous conduit à l'interprétation tragique de ses comédies ou si c'est l'interprétation tragique de

[1] P. Brisson, *Molière, sa vie dans ses œuvres*, 1939, pp. 29, 151. Molière's English biographers (Trollope, Tilley, Palmer) seem outstandingly sane on this point. Cf. especially Tilley, *Molière*, 1921, pp. 19–20, and J. Palmer, *Molière: His Life and Works*, 1931, ch. xiii. Palmer remarks (p. 185) that Beffara's discovery 'far from terminating the controversy, only added to its complexity. Its astounding convolutions during the next hundred years are only explicable on the assumption that there is an unconscious human bias in favour of scandalous readings.' We must indeed not expect to settle by any single document a controversy so thorny. The morals of strolling actors were to our judgement astonishingly loose, and it may be true that Molière later passed off his daughter as Madeleine's sister. But it is scientifically unpardonable to assume it true or to assert that the evidence is sufficient to lend weight to such an assumption.

ses comédies qui nous entraîne à supposer la tragédie dans son existence.'[1] The corollary of this is that the plays are free from interpretation as camouflaged biography; they are free for aesthetic analysis. If, for instance, *L'École des Maris* need no longer be interpreted (in the manner of Abel Lefranc) so that the clue to its understanding is 'la passion très vive qu'il [Molière] éprouvait à ce moment pour Armande',[2] one is free to discover a comic theme developed according to the laws of stagecraft.

It is Michaut's great merit, then, to have cleared the ground. That does not mean that his own interpretations of his author still command assent. His volumes are works of literary science, even more than of biography. He presents each play as a literary work, analysing its content, marshalling the evidence concerning its success on the stage, discussing its implications. Yet he attempts an interpretation of the plays on the basis of the known facts about the plays, a method which might well impress such a student of Sainte-Beuve as M. Michaut had shown himself to be. The aesthetic principle involved in the comedy tends to be preferred to exterior data, explaining the 'meaning' of a work by what is known of its 'milieu' and its 'moment'. Scholars are now turning away from this confusion of external and internal data.[3] A case in point is perhaps *Don Juan*, a play of which M. Michaut seeks the meaning in the aura of libertinage surrounding its theme and in which (significantly) he sees no comedy. But to do this is to repeat what has been so disastrous for *Tartuffe* and to attempt the vain and impossible task

[1] *Jeunesse de Molière*, p. 14. Cf. Mornet, op. cit., p. 273: 'En fait nous ne savons rien du caractère réel de Molière.' Many English editors seem to hold the contrary view.

[2] Michaut, *Les Débuts* . . . , p. 128, where six other scholars are quoted as holding similar views. Fernandez, in his short biography (1929), takes essentially, but more intelligently, the same line (pp. 106–10).

[3] Cf. L. Jouvet in *Conferencia*, 1937, p. 286: 'Ce n'est pas par la vie d'un homme qu'on explique ses œuvres.' And a remarkable page of criticism in Hytier, *André Gide*, 1945, p. 3.

of explaining comedy as satire. If we think that Molière is exposing to ridicule a certain attitude, we shall read the play with different
eyes from those who see it as a study in relationships that produce
comedy.[1]

To understand Molière's intention we must not import into any
given play views which Molière might have held had he (which is
doubtful) learnt his philosophy from Gassendi. We should do
better to study the dramatic tradition in which he was working and
to realize that any expression of personal views was possibly far
from his mind. This line has been followed by several scholars and
recent general works show how fruitful it has proved.[2] The most
original work of this nature was done almost half a century ago by
Lanson. In a remarkable study he traced Molière's affinities with
contemporary farce and with the Italian *commedia dell' arte*. Lanson
showed how important for a real understanding of Molière's plays
was the fact that he was trained to act in a mask, that Mascarille was
by nomenclature a masked character, and that much of the fixity
imposed by the mask clings to such creations as Alceste and Tartuffe.
It is significant that these views have been recently enforced by more
than one actor who has studied Molière after having produced or
played in his comedies.[3]

French farce has always borne a rich crop of satiric intention, and
it is obvious that Molière made full use of this. How far he was prepared to go in ridiculing features of his time and country is a fascinating and unsolved problem. It has been well said that a good part
of the audiences who found Arnolphe funny shared his views on

[1] The comic aspect of the libertine would seem to be the contrast between
apparent superiority to other men's ideals and the humanity whereby he shares
the common lot, in life and in death. The poetic counterpart of this, which is
also comic in itself, is the dependence of the clever master on the stupid valet.
(Cf. *infra*, p. 96.)

[2] Notably H. C. Lancaster, *History of French Dramatic Literature in the
Seventeenth Century*, Part III: The Period of Molière. Johns Hopkins, 2 vols.,
1936.

[3] G. Lanson, 'Molière et la farce', *Revue de Paris*, 1901, pp. 129–53.

youth more than they shared those of his youthful antagonists. There are views on the education of women in the *École*, but it is not a pamphlet. It is the work of a man who could make a dramatic character at once both realistic and ridiculous, who could moreover make control of youth seem ridiculous even to those who believed in it. A still earlier play presents an even more intriguing mosaic of social criticism and comic attitude, *Les Précieuses Ridicules*. It has fared so variously at the hands of the critics that it provides a good illustration both of what has been achieved and of what still awaits attention in the field of Molière study. Though slight, it is recognized as important early evidence of Molière's comic manner. (Was it not Diderot who warned us against thinking that more men were able to write *Pourceaugnac* than *Le Misanthrope*?) Yet even to-day there exists no critical edition, either French or foreign, nor any collation, on scientific principles, of the data necessary to the student who wishes to discover how much of it is criticism of actual social conditions and how much is the development of a comic situation which needs none but the slenderest basis of reality.

In the mid-nineteenth century Victor Cousin expounded his theory that *Les Précieuses Ridicules* was an attack, not on the real 'précieuses' but on their pale and artificial imitators. Lanson maintained some fifty years later[1] that the available evidence pointed to the conclusion that Molière was indeed attacking 'la vraie préciosité, celle de l'Hôtel de Rambouillet'. He explained the play as the satire of a typical bourgeois against aristocratic elegance: Molière, he wrote, 'nous propose l'idéal le plus bourgeois de la vie paisible d'affections domestiques. Il y a de plus hautes morales.' Later still came the idea that Molière had not only attacked the 'précieuses' but had defeated them and had killed affectation, or at least had laughed it out of court to such an extent that the final blow of *Les Femmes Savantes* in 1672 brought about what Michaut calls 'le discrédit total des précieuses'. All these positions are now either queried or

[1] *Les Précieuses Ridicules*, ed. Lanson, n.d.

B

rejected. The most recent theory[1] accounts for the awkward gap of a fortnight between the first two performances by marshalling the arguments for an original version not only more satirical than what we now read, but harsh and gross as well. Adam has at least shown that the social background of the play is much more complicated than either Cousin or Lanson supposed, that social cliques opposed each other in the Paris of 1659 with much of the animosity of the political intrigues of the Fronde, that in particular the circle surrounding Gaston d'Orléans and the Grande Mademoiselle, forming a powerful and licentious coterie, included Molière's friends, d'Aubignac, Boileau, Cotin (not yet an enemy), and that a corresponding group around Fouquet included his enemies, or the enemies of his friends Ménage, Mlle de Scudéry, Pellisson, Sorel. An actor-manager fresh from the provinces might well show his mettle and court advancement by taking one side against the other and the d'Aubignac party might well demand a satire as indecent as it was merciless. It is plausible again that after an 'alcoviste de qualité', obviously in touch with Fouquet, had succeeded in getting the play off the boards after one performance, Molière should make a bold bid to conciliate the party he had been persuaded to lampoon, should not only tone down his play but should perform its new and acceptable version in the house of Mme du Plessis-Guénégaud, as indeed happened. Adam's fascinating study suggests a Molière less dignified and more natural than the official account. It has received some measure of corroboration from an unusual quarter. In a resounding article, which unfortunately appeared only in an out-of-the-way periodical, M. Daniel Mornet has questioned all the accepted ideas on preciosity as a social phenomenon.[2] All too easily

[1] A. Adam, 'La Genèse des Précieuses ridicules', *Revue d'histoire et de philosophie*, Lille, 1939, pp. 1–46. But see also H. Cottez, ibid., 1943, pp. 340–64.

[2] D. Mornet, 'La Signification et l'évolution de l'idée de préciosité en France au 17ᵉ siècle', *Journal of the History of Ideas*, i (1940), pp. 225–31. The conclusions of this article are embodied in Mornet, op. cit., pp. 25–44.

in the past, he says, has the mockery of Boileau and Molière been taken as evidence of the actual existence of affectation such as they, and Somaize in their train, describe. Thanks to this confusion 'on a reconstitué une histoire de la préciosité qui n'a à peu près rien à voir avec la réalité'. There is evidence of affectation, in both language and manners, about 1640. There is no evidence that the ladies called 'les précieuses' in 1659 spoke absurdly or indulged in anything more affected than elegant and platonic discussion: 'il n'y en a pas qui aient parlé comme Cathos et Madelon.' Nor finally is there any evidence that such circles were affected, much less discredited, by Molière's plays: 'Quand on étudie non pas les chefs-d'œuvre mais l'ensemble de la littérature, on est frappé de voir que les critiques de Molière et de Boileau ont été comme si elles n'existaient pas.'

After this, it would be difficult to assert that Molière scholarship has not reached an interesting stage. It looks as if the texts used in our schools and universities, far from being hackneyed and 'exhausted', are only just beginning to yield up their secrets. There is already enough new material on many plays of Molière for the enterprising teacher to renew his own approach to the subject and to inspire keen students with a quite new notion as to what the French classical movement really was.[1]

It would not, I think, be accurate to describe recent work on *Les Précieuses Ridicules* as concerned only with the social background of the play. It concentrates attention on the dramatic nature of Molière's production. We are warned not to look for the wrong things; the plays are not reliable social satire, in the first place, any more than they are (in the first place) dramatized versions of Molière's home life; they are comedies, and until we have discovered what seventeenth-century actors put into their plays we shall not know how distorted is Molière's picture of preciosity, or of medical practice, or of religion in his own day. The positive counterpart to

[1] Cf. H. Peyre, *Le Classicisme français*, New York, 1942; D. Mornet, op. cit.; nd A. Barbier, 'L'École de 1660', *French Studies*, i. 1. 27–36.

the work of Adam and Mornet on Molière's first Paris play has already been supplied by Ramon Fernandez, who suggests that affectation gave Molière a chance of making dramatic and comic contrast with something vigorous, matter of fact, ebullient, earthy, even coarse, Rabelaisian.

'Le langage précieux est une manière d'éviter de toucher les choses en évitant de leur donner leur nom usuel; le code sentimental des précieuses est une manière d'éviter de toucher les corps, les corps de ces hommes "vraiment nus" contre lesquels Cathos et Madelon ne veulent point coucher. Hommes et mots "vraiment nus", voilà ce que la préciosité — celle de Cathos comme celle d'Armande, comme celle, plus subtile et provisoire, de Célimène — repousse et recouvre d'un voile, que Molière déchire avec une rage allègre. Non par raison et bon sens, comme on l'a dit assez superficiellement, mais pour satisfaire un instinct impérieux et gourmand, une hâte des sens et des muscles qui fait de lui l'ennemi en quelque sorte biologique des superfétations.'[1]

Recent work has explored other plays in the same direction. The studies of Arnavon, for example, have shown the abundance of vigorous comedy in *L'École des Femmes*, *Le Misanthrope*, and *Le Malade*. Gutkind has done the same for *L'Avare* and Reynier for *Les Femmes Savantes*.[2] Jouvet has brought powerful support to the view of Molière as primarily an actor-author, driven to express in dramatic form, not pills of moral platitude with a comic coating, but a truly poetic imagination. 'Molière, qu'on a étiqueté l'homme de la raison, est l'homme qui a le mieux senti et le mieux compris ce que c'était que le déraisonnable, et son théâtre, qui paraît être le triomphe de la raison aux yeux de ses commentateurs, est surtout en vérité le royaume de cette merveilleuse déraison qui s'appelle la poésie.' And in a later article: 'Derrière Molière, qui est le premier

[1] *Tableau de la littérature française de Corneille à Chénier*, 1939, pp. 79–99.

[2] J. Arnavon, *L'Interprétation de la comédie classique: Le Misanthrope*, 1930; *L'École des Femmes*, 1936; *Le Malade Imaginaire*, 1938. C. S. Gutkind, *Molière und das komische Drama*, 1928; G. Reynier, *Les Femmes Savantes de Molière*, n.d.

de tous, tous ses héros sont des imaginaires ou des imaginatifs, des hommes en proie à eux-mêmes, des déraisonnables qui raisonnent dans la déraison.'[1] This view has found less paradoxical and more detailed expression in the work of Valdemar Vedel, one chapter of which traces the force and range of this comic aptitude ('le démon du théâtre') which led Molière not only to dramatize situations and ideas by representing them through contrasted characters, but even to make his actors assume parts and impose themselves as other than they are: 'Comédiens, ils le sont tous: Tartuffe comme Célimène, le bel esprit idéaliste comme l'arrogant philosophe. Les plus impudents ont de la joie à nous laisser deviner ce qu'ils cachent sous leur masque, mais sans jamais le quitter tout à fait.'[2]

The tendency, in the strict sense of the word, in this new work is a return to Molière the dramatist. Where older critics saw either the satirist or the subjective poet, more recent scholars seek the artist and technician of comedy. The tendency is not confined to Molière. The plays of his great contemporary Corneille have been explained, not on the traditional lines of the glorification of the will, or as studies in psychology, but as 'machines to create emotion' in an audience.[3] This new attitude implies that the plays must be read as plays and not as propaganda, that for example we are only entitled to find in them Molière's own view about the golden mean or humane religion once we have determined the *dramatic* value of the passages concerned. What in many cases has been ascribed to Molière's ideas may be the expression of a point of view necessary to complete the dramatic contrast. This does not say that Molière's drama is not full of ideas, or that it does not transmit a view of life. But the view of life, the *Weltanschauung*, is not where scholars have been too ready to find it, lying scattered on the surface, in the speeches of the most 'reasonable' and often least dramatic character

[1] *Conferencia*, 1937, p. 282; 1938, p. 662.
[2] V. Vedel, *Corneille et son temps. Molière*, 1935, p. 435.
[3] J. Boorsch, in *Yale Romanic Studies*, xviii (1941), pp. 101 ff.

in any given play, but is hidden deep in the philosophical conception of the whole dramatic situation.[1]

The whole question of what Molière believed has therefore to be gone into afresh. To state the question thus is in itself misleading, since the only evidence must be the plays legitimately interpreted, and comic drama may very well provide little clue as to what its author 'believed'. Rightly understood, however, that drama may tell us much about the nature of its creator's mind. The change of view comes out well if one compares two sets of statements. For Perrens, writing in 1899, 'Molière est libertin jusqu'aux moelles . . . on pourrait dire le seul agressif.'[2] Similarly Lefranc wrote in 1905: 'L'influence de Gassendi sur Molière ne saurait être contestée.'[3] With these compare Thibaudet's statement that 'Molière n'a d'autre philosophie que l'art de dénoncer, de rendre sensibles, l'automatisme et la raideur, et d'en faire rire',[4] and Arnavon's useful collection of the views on all kinds of questions that can be found in Molière's comedy: 'Le vaste monde que Molière a mis sur la scène et doué d'un prodigieux pouvoir de renouvellement s'offre depuis trois siècles au jugement des hommes.'[5] There is no doubt about a change in emphasis.

Some very delicate questions await treatment here. What for example is the 'meaning' of *L'École des Femmes*? It is a comedy 'à thèse', said Brunetière. What is the thesis? A return to nature, as some have thought, or almost the opposite? 'Le fond de sa pensée est qu'il faut faire l'éducation de la primitive nature.' Each of the great plays of Molière raises questions of this kind. The study of

[1] Cf. E. Wechsler, *Molière als Philosoph*, 1910. More helpful are Meredith, *An Essay on Comedy and the Uses of the Comic Spirit*, 1877, and Samuel Alexander, *Molière and Life*, 1926.

[2] *Les Libertins en France*, 1899, p. 342.

[3] Cit. Michaut, *Jeunesse*, p. 69 n. Michaut's treatment of the whole question (pp. 67–95) is worth reading.

[4] 'Le Rire de Molière', *Revue de Paris*, 1922, pp. 312–33.

[5] J. Arnavon, *Morale de Molière*, 1945, p. 7. Cf. his suggestive earlier book, *Molière notre contemporain*, 1929.

Molière as one of the supreme manifestations of the modern spirit is perhaps in its preliminary stage. Fernandez suggests a basis for further advance: 'L'interprétation comique du monde implique une vision qui implique à son tour une philosophie. . . . On peut écrire *Scapin* ou *Sganarelle* sans changer l'ordre intellectuel du monde. Cela n'est plus possible quand on écrit *Tartuffe* et *Le Misanthrope*.'[1] Before any synthesis is possible we need the studies of single plays, of *Don Juan*, for example, in which the peculiar type of comic understanding has so far been as good as neglected in favour of the satire and the ideas connected with the traditional treatment of its famous theme.[2] We need more investigation of *George Dandin*, on which Gutkind has a very suggestive outline study, of *Le Malade Imaginaire*, following in the trail blazed by Arnavon. Patient analysis of language and dramatic 'motifs' within the latter play may help to elucidate why it is regarded by André Gide as 'la plus neuve, la plus hardie, la plus belle' of all Molière's masterpieces, achieving 'une grandeur que le théâtre n'a jamais dépassée'.[3] Such analysis would, I suggest, have to show how far the subject exceeds mere satire of doctors, how the scenes are built on the profoundly human interplay of illusion and reality. Argan is the man who is well until he *thinks* he is ill, a poetic symbol surely of the dichotomy of being and thinking ('Tenez, Monsieur, vous ne songez pas que vous ne sauriez marcher sans bâton'). The analysis of this 'imagination', as Jouvet has suggested, appears constantly in Molière and is not peculiar to his work. Pascal's words[4] show a similar awareness of the human

---

[1] Fernandez, op. cit., p. 86. Cf. Mornet, op. cit., p. 271: 'il n'est pas douteux que Molière . . . a, non pas prêché, mais suggéré une morale toute laïque, qui était au fond d'elle-même la contradiction de la morale chrétienne.'

[2] Cf. Arnavon, *Le Don Juan de Molière*, Copenhagen, 1947.

[3] *Journal*, 1939–42, pp. 132–4.

[4] Wrongly deciphered by Brunschvicg (Ed. minor, p. 362) and corrected by Z. Tourneur (Éditions de Cluny, 1938, i. 12): 'Imagination. C'est cette partie dominante dans l'homme, cause de tous les déportements, cette maîtresse d'erreur et de fausseté. . . . Je ne parle pas des fous, je parle des plus sages et c'est parmi eux que l'imagination a le grand droit de persuader les hommes.'

tendency to conceive things other than as they are. This opens up a field of comedy of a subtler kind than the deliberate schemes of rogues and fools like Tartuffe, Harpagon, Arnolphe, or Don Juan, all of whom strive to make others see them as they are not. The comedy of those who get things wrong, Dandin, Alceste, Argan, is perhaps of a different order. It approaches sublimity in the person of Alceste,[1] who is scandalized because things are not as they should be, and who confuses, in his doctrinaire idealism, it has been said, 'Wahrheit' and 'Wirklichkeit'.[2] Such a statement as 'J'ai pour moi la justice et je perds mon procès' opens poetic vistas which transcend any immediate comic effect.

Such studies might well prepare an attack on another great unsolved question of Molière criticism, his conception of the comic. So many critics, particularly Anglo-Saxon, speak of the things in Molière which are not comic. Let us first see whether the French share our notion of comedy. We find it, for example, unnatural to admit that comedy may go far below the surface of human nature; that the comic attitude may penetrate to the heart of things we are reluctant to believe. But the French may well do so, and Molière may well have done so. Before agreeing with Goethe (who was badly reported in any case) that *L'Avare* is more tragic than comic, let us see whether Molière's comic vision did not include the tragic and the sinister and the bitter. Bergson's analysis[3] suggests that for the Latin mind comedy is a view of human relationships, which may well be profound, in which the specifically human is opposed by some form of automatism. As Thibaudet has argued, the angle from which Tartuffe is regarded is not so much 'laideur' as 'raideur'. Harpagon is defined, by a victim, as one of those 'naturels rétifs que

---

[1] Cf. Prof. G. Rudler's recent edition of the play (Oxford, Blackwell, 1947).

[2] Gutkind, op. cit., pp. 112 ff.

[3] Cf. *Laughter*, Eng. trans., 1911, p. 146: 'What is essentially laughable is what is done automatically. In a vice, even in a virtue, the comic is that element by which the person unwittingly betrays himself.'

la vérité fait cabrer, qui toujours se raidissent contre le droit chemin de la raison'. Don Juan, says a critic already quoted, 'se raidit jusque devant la mort'. Perhaps Tartuffe would supply a supreme example of this 'raideur' which (but for his gross sensuality) would be completely inhuman.[1]

If this approach can be substantiated by further study we may advance our knowledge of the technique of the comic dramatist who perceives the gap ('écart') between life and thought, reality and notions, and as an artist brings together cases where they clash most sharply, and which by the very suddenness of the opposition provoke laughter. A last quotation will show that this line of investigation has also been sketched out. Fernandez again, to whom are due so many incentives to a new view of comedy, analyses the famous scene from *Le Bourgeois Gentilhomme* in which the professional philosopher loses his temper, and shows how laughter is produced by the juxtaposition of contraries and how the choice of these contraries is a result not only of imagination but of an intellectual judgement on life.

'Le lien logique entre la théorie contre la colère et la colère dans *Le Bourgeois Gentilhomme* est la projection du jugement de Molière. Il substitue au désordre de la vie l'ordre d'une réflexion qui rassemble de multiples observations éparses. L'événement n'obéit plus aux lois de la vie, tout en conservant les apparences, mais aux lois de la raison. Le rapport ridicule de cause à effet est une opération de l'esprit qui s'insère dans le réel, comme une main dans une marionnette, pour lui donner la forme du jugement.'[2]

If this be true, Molière is much more than a talented observer of human nature. He seems rather to portray human behaviour with

---

[1] The conception of humanity would seem to me to be the key to that of the comic. The comic figure is redeemed from complete inhumanity by the fatal irruption into his *ingenious* scheme of his unsuspected *natural* qualities. Laughter arises only when the contrast between these two comes to the surface, but the contrast itself lies deep in human nature.

[2] Fernandez, op. cit., p. 90.

the imagination of an artist, and in so doing to suggest a judgement on that behaviour. A door is thus opened to interpretations of his drama which, should they prove sound, would revolutionize the teaching at present given in our schools.[1]

[1] The most recent compendium of knowledge for the student or teacher is D. Mornet, *Molière*, 1943, in the series Le Livre de l'Étudiant. See also R. Jasinski, *Le Misanthrope de Molière*, 1951, and D. Romeno, *Essai sur le comique de Molière*, 1951. René Bray's last book, *Molière homme de théâtre*, Mercure de France, 1954, is useful and suggestive. It contains evidence (on p. 95) that Molière actually played the rôle of Mascarille *in a mask* in Paris in 1661.

II. MIME

PERHAPS the most obvious thing to say about Molière is just that he was an actor. It was as such that he was first, and chiefly, known to his contemporaries. It was for acting rather than for reading that he composed his plays. It would seem natural therefore to begin the study of Molière's work from this professional angle. Yet such has not so far been the case. The evidence concerning the actual art on the stage of 'le premier farceur de France' has never been assembled or discussed. May it not prove that passages otherwise obscure find a plain and natural explanation in the fact that they conform, not to any abstract code of aesthetics, but to the demands of a repertory company? The present chapter is an attempt to present, and then to evaluate, the evidence. So distinguished an actor as M. Louis Jouvet has complained that the academic theories of Molière scholars are of no use to the actor seeking an interpretation of the main roles, and that, despite two hundred and fifty years of criticism, we are still forced to stand in uncomprehending bewilderment ('désarroi') before his work.

It is interesting that what is possibly the earliest reference to Molière as actor speaks of him also as an undergraduate. The fragment bears no date, and is in the form of a note appended by

Tallemant des Réaux to his paragraph on La Béjard.[1] It runs as follows:

'Un garçon nommé Molière quitta les bancs de Sorbonne pour la suivre; il en fut longtemps amoureux, donnait des avis à la troupe, et enfin s'en mit et l'épousa. Il a fait des pièces où il y a de l'esprit. Ce n'est pas un merveilleux acteur, si ce n'est pour le ridicule. Il n'y a que sa troupe qui joue ses pièces; elles sont comiques.'

The passage is clearly gossip, like most of Tallemant, albeit faithfully reported. One could hardly imagine so industrious a collector not knowing more about Molière after, shall we say, the success and polemic of the *École des Femmes*, so the information would seem to date from 1662 at the latest. It is in several respects inaccurate. There is no likelihood that Molière did study at the Sorbonne, and he certainly did not marry Madeleine Béjard. But on the matter of his acting, Tallemant would appear to be giving the general opinion. Molière played many tragic parts and was famous in none. Some years after his death the daughter of his fellow actor Du Croisy explained this fact as due to his physique being unsuited for tragic acting. Contemporaries had certainly made fun of it and had provoked sharp rejoinders on Molière's own stage. Mascarille is astonished that the 'Précieuses' ask him to which actors he will give the play he has written. 'Belle demande. Aux grands comédiens; il n'y a qu'eux qui soient capables de faire valoir les choses; les autres sont des ignorants qui récitent comme l'on parle; ils ne savent pas faire ronfler les vers et s'arrêter au bel endroit.' Four years later the thrust was repeated, and rammed home by actual mimicry. In *L'Impromptu de Versailles* Molière portrays himself as reproving a young colleague who recites lines from *Nicomède* 'le plus naturellement qu'il lui aurait été possible': 'Comment, vous appelez cela réciter? C'est se railler. Il faut dire les choses avec emphase. Écoutez-moi . . .' and he proceeds to ridicule the 'emphase', and lack of natural diction, of five of his contemporaries at the Hôtel.

[1] *Historiettes*, ed. Mongrédien, vii. 127.

The point at issue between Molière and his rivals seems to have been more than one of pique at his failure to score success in tragic parts. His attempt to make tragic diction more 'natural' seems to have been too much for contemporary taste, which wanted tragedy to be almost intoned, or at any rate declaimed with a solemnity removed from ordinary speech. His irony in referring to them as 'les grands comédiens' was itself ironical since the public, in spite of all that Molière could do or say, continued to think that the acting at the Hôtel was 'proper acting'. Perhaps for such a reason the young Racine removed his *Alexandre* from Molière's theatre. There is certainly evidence to support Molière's defence of a new and natural diction. Tallemant, as we have seen, admits that in funny plays he was very successful. Two of his own actors, paying tribute to him nine years after his death, make much of his skill in 'le jeu naïf du théâtre'. Their description has peculiar authority:

'Il n'était pas seulement inimitable dans la manière dont il soutenait tous les caractères de ses comédies; mais il leur donnait encore un agrément tout particulier par la justesse qui accompagnait le jeu des acteurs: un coup-d'œil, un pas, un geste, tout y était observé avec une exactitude qui avait été inconnue jusque là sur les théâtres de Paris.'

It would seem that Molière, whether or not he was disappointed at failing to succeed as an actor of tragedy, established for the theatre-going public of mid-seventeenth-century Paris a new style of acting, in which he not only himself excelled but succeeded in training his company. Whereas the dominant tradition of his day insisted on declamation as the mark of good acting, Molière seems from the first to have essayed something not only more ordinary but much nearer mimicry. It is referred to by epithets such as 'naturel', 'naïf', 'justesse', 'observé avec exactitude'. Should one not conclude from this that the 'realism' we find in the plays is the outcome not of poetic or satiric intention, or of literary attitude, but of a type of acting which proved successful in practice? That it was successful was due no doubt not merely to Molière's personal talent but to the taste of the public, of that cultivated public which about 1660 seemed to appreciate the 'natural'.[1]

> Maintenant il ne faut pas
> Quitter la nature d'un pas.

So commented La Fontaine, perhaps after he had seen Molière act.

Traces of this taste for, and skill in portraying, the 'natural' can be found in all Molière's plays. He used to the full the comic tradition of ordinary gesture and situation. The physical is everywhere in its own right and very often symbolical of the moral. Sosie's cowardice is conveyed by his stammer, Sganarelle's excitement by a tumble, Harpagon's universal suspicion by his comments on the actual audience in front of him. *L'Avare* is full of concrete illustrations of moral qualities; nothing is described, everything is shown in and by physical act: Harpagon searches his man's clothes, runs after his money, wears glasses and a ring on his finger, crawls under the table. Are not these but the mummified remains of what was once alive and spontaneous in 'le jeu naïf du théâtre'? Even congealed in the text they are calculated to rejoice the heart of the actor seeking to live a part.

Admitting that Molière was a brilliant exponent of 'le jeu naïf', is it possible to discover whether he invented a method to suit his gifts, or took over a tradition other than that of his tragic rivals? A little research proves that, like other men of genius, Molière was attaching himself to something already established rather than creating a completely new medium. Both the performance and the theme of seventeenth-century French tragedy, for example, go back to a Renaissance revival of the academic productions of medieval students. One medium of seventeenth-century comedy goes back to the same movement; one may think of Corneille, for instance, as writing comedies in a style perfected by Larivey and others on the model revived by Jodelle. Molière has other and more earthy roots. It was not for nothing that he was called a *farceur*. The name was an accurate description not merely of the sort of play he preferred

[1] Cf. Madelon in *Les Précieuses Ridicules*: 'Que tout ce qu'il dit est naturel.'

but of his style and tradition of acting. For the tradition of the
French farce had never lost its popularity, though it had rarely
achieved respectability. It was in this tradition, as M. Lanson showed
us forty years ago, that Molière was trained and that his own powers
developed. From the indecent *gauloiserie* of the farce to the elegance of *Le Misanthrope* may seem a far cry, yet both are in the
same literary tradition. It is clear even to the outsider that Molière
discarded much, and grafted entirely new elements on to what he
kept. It is the task of scholarship to find out how much was kept,
and the vital factor to have in mind when studying his choice is that
he was as much, and as instinctively, an actor as he was an author.

Most of the evidence of Molière's early contacts with farce has
been lost. We do not know what farces he watched, or played in, or
wrote, or adapted, before 1658. He may as a boy have watched the
famous Tabarin. It would be strange if a boy of his temperament
had not made early acquaintance with Gros René, Gaultier Garguille,
Floridor, and Jodelet. On the other hand, we have evidence of his contacts with the farces played by the Italian actors of the *commedia dell'
arte*. His enemies reproached him for having been their too servile
disciple. The skit of 1670 called *Élomire Hypocondre* contains (in
the judgement of M. Michaut) more than a little actual biography.
This upstart of the stage presumes to attain perfection in a new
art:

> Veut se rendre parfait dans l'art de faire rire,
> Que fait-il, le matois, dans ce hardi dessein?
> Chez le grand Scaramouche il va soir et matin,
> Là le miroir en main et ce grand homme en face,
> Il n'est contorsion, posture ni grimace
> Que ce grand écolier du plus grand des bouffons
> Ne fasse et ne refasse en cent et cent façons.
> Tantôt pour exprimer les soucis d'un ménage,
> De mille et mille plis il fronce son visage;
> Puis, joignant la pâleur à ces rides qu'il fait,
> D'un mari malheureux il est le vrai portrait.

The arrow is barbed by a frontispiece, still to be seen in the copy in the Arsenal Library, but said to have been destroyed by Molière's efforts in all the others, showing the Italian master, whip in hand, making gestures, copied by the pupil holding a mirror, and the legend: 'Qualis erit tanto docente magistro?'

This testimony is later confirmed by Tralage, who had no axe to grind, and was probably merely noting what he found to be common knowledge: 'Molière estimait fort Scaramouche pour ses manières naturelles; il le voyait fort souvent et il lui a servi pour former les meilleurs acteurs de sa troupe.' (Among the characters in *L'Avare* occurs the name of Brindavoine, another of Scaramouche's favourite pupils.)

The farce and the *commedia dell' arte* clearly had much in common and it is not now, I think, possible to determine what Molière owed to each.[1] Both were played in masks. Both relied on the realistic and even gross presentation of a few set types, such as the old man, the pedant, the valet, and the nurse. The *commedia* as played in Paris after 1650 had probably lost many of its original features, such as the partition of roles to suit the various Italian dialects. One suggestion is that it differed from the farce in dealing with imaginative caricature rather than earthy reality. But perhaps the main difference was that it had few or no written parts. Its actors were trained to improvise and embroider a 'canevas' or skeleton of plot, and thus to rely more on mime than on speech. The fact that they played to audiences largely ignorant of their own tongue no doubt enforced this practice. An Italian actor of Molière's own day has left evidence that brings out the extreme importance of this fact:

'Les comédiens italiens n'apprennent rien par cœur; il leur suffit pour jouer une comédie d'en avoir vu le sujet un moment avant que d'entrer sur le théâtre. . . . Qui dit "bon comédien italien" dit un homme qui a du fond, qui joue plus d'imagination que de mémoire, qui marie si bien ses

---

[1] Cf., however, some interesting suggestions in the article by A. Gill on 'The Doctor in the Farce and Molière', *French Studies*, ii. 2, April 1948.

actions à ses paroles, avec celles de son camarade, qu'il entre sur le champ dans tout le jeu et dans tous les mouvements que l'autre lui demande, de manière à faire croire qu'ils s'étaient déjà concertés.'[1]

Clearly the Italian practice expected more from the actor and evoked more remarkable power than the native French tradition. Such men as Biancolelli (died 1688) as Arlequin, and Fiorelli (died 1694) as Scaramouche, provided a standard of acting to which no French contemporaries (before Molière) could approach.

This suppleness demanded of the actor seems at first sight to accord ill with the rigidity of character associated with the farce and in particular with the mask, which was the chief mark of the actor, known in advance and intended to be recognized at once. But there is little doubt that here too Molière conformed to, and learnt much from, the farcical tradition. He was trained to act in a mask, he probably did so in at least one Paris play. The name Mascarille ('little mask') suggests this, an engraving of 1666 also does, and a text of 1663 supplies corroborative evidence: 'Il contrefaisait d'abord les Marquis avec le masque de Mascarille; il n'osait les jouer autrement; mais à la fin il nous a fait voir qu'il avait le visage assez plaisant pour représenter sans masque un personnage ridicule.'[2] Details of roles played in masks support this assertion that Molière did not use it for long. *Les Fourberies de Scapin*, when revived in 1736, had the old men played in masks but not Scapin himself. According to Guy Patin, who had every chance to know and no inducement to lie, the doctors in *L'Amour Médecin* were masked. Lulli the musician performed parts in *Monsieur de Pourceaugnac* and *Le Bourgeois Gentilhomme*, both with the mask. The native counterpart to the mask seems to have been heavy clown's make-up. Jodelet in the *Précieuses* was thus 'enfariné'. One gathers that the 'flour' was not so much for scenic as for farcical effect. Sauval

---

[1] Évariste Gherardi, cit. P. L. Duchartre, *La Comédie italienne*, 1924.

[2] Villiers, *Réponse à l'Impromptu de Versailles*, 1663. Cit. G. Doutrepont, *Les Acteurs masqués et enfarinés en France*, 1926, p. 16.

speaks of an actor who 'ne portait point de masque, mais se couvrait le visage de farine, et ménageait cette farine de sorte qu'en remuant seulement un peu les lèvres il blanchissait tout d'un coup ceux qui lui parlaient'.[1]

The mask has some claim to represent the oldest of all European traditions of acting. Gilbert Murray has written that 'it is significant that both in Greek and in Latin the word for mask is also the word for character; and Dramatis Personae means, strictly speaking, "the masks needed in the performance". The cross elderly uncle had one sort of mask, the indulgent elderly uncle another. The Obstinate Man, the Flatterer, the Bragging Soldier and the Modest Soldier were got up in such a way that the audience could recognise each type, whatever his name or adventures might be.'[2] But here at all events is Molière's starting-point. The mask performed a double service. It freed the actor and it fixed the character. By making the actor anonymous it allowed him to fool to the top of his bent without fear of giving offence. In the sixteenth century it was said that 'nous voyons les Comediens italiens masquer leur Pantalon et leur Zani de Jehan Cornet à fin de plus hardiment jouer, et se moquer, car le masque ne rougit point'. But even more important than this liberty of the actor was the fixity of his role, ensuring that all his efforts were bent to fulfil a clear conception, a definite character. And it seems that Molière the dramatist started from, and indeed in essentials kept close to, this conception of character as fixed. 'Molière a conçu d'abord le caractère sous la forme du masque italien que les farceurs français s'étaient approprié. . . . Arnolphe, Harpagon, Tartuffe, Alceste ont ce trait du masque italien de porter à travers toutes les situations de la pièce la fixité invariable de leur caractère . . . la permanence de leur type est éclatante et inaltérable.' Such are the words of M. Lanson's famous article, confirmed by

[1] Doutrepont, op. cit., p. 32.
[2] *New Chapters in the History of Greek Literature*, 2nd series, Oxford, 1929, p. 22.

much recent investigation and easily verifiable. One can hardly fail to notice that in Molière's dramas there are, as one scholar puts it, no conversions.[1] The great characters may be sobered by misfortune, but they leave the play very much as they entered it, unaltered in essentials. This has been welcomed as proof that Molière, as we say, remains true to life. But English students must beware here. The cliché is deceptive. These impressive figures may give us the illusion of life, but variety and individuality are not the keynotes of his drama. The keyword is rather clarity. It is French drama.

Consideration of the mask as symbol would lead us to the animating principle of comedy as Molière evolved it, and the discussion goes beyond the framework of a chapter on Molière as actor. But it is interesting to notice his fondness for a quite different type of situation, in which he could drop the mask and appear, on the stage, in his own character and with his own name. The attraction of that delightful green-room scene, *L'Impromptu de Versailles*, lies in the appearance of a company of actors as they really were, in everyday costume and occupation, Molière playing the harassed role of actor-manager that needed no rehearsing. The same trick—is it not an actor's fancy?—opened the performance of the *Fâcheux* in 1661 and is thus described in the Preface:

'D'abord que la toile fut levée, un des acteurs, comme vous pourriez dire moi, parut sur le théâtre en habit de ville, et s'adressant au roi avec le visage d'un homme surpris, fit des excuses en désordre sur ce qu'il se trouvoit là seul, et manquoit de temps et d'acteurs pour donner à Sa Majesté le divertissement qu'elle sembloit attendre. En même temps au milieu de vingt jets d'eau naturels, s'ouvrit cette coquille que tout le monde a vue; et l'agréable naïade qui parut dedans s'avança au bord du

[1] A. Bailly, *L'École classique française*, p. 53. It is only fair to quote the passage, since the conclusion does not seem to me to follow from the statement: 'Il n'y a pas de conversions dans son théâtre et c'est par là qu'il est le plus vrai. Un pessimisme inébranlable forme l'assise de ses comédies, et le vers de Musset est juste. . . . Alceste est puni de sa vertu farouche, mais la rigueur du sort ne peut qu'accroître sa misanthropie, Harpagon ne vivra plus que pour sa cassette. . . .' The point is more justly made by Vedel, op. cit., p. 437.

théâtre, et d'un air héroïque prononça les vers que M. Pellisson avoit faits et qui servent de prologue.'

This charming note gives a glimpse of the informality and co-opera-tive effort that preceded the 'divertissements' for which Molière became famous. A third and quite distinct example of the actor bringing himself into the play is the discussion in *Le Malade Imaginaire*. That Argan, played by Molière, should shake with rage over 'that fellow Molière' and prophesy his end was in itself a brilliant dramatic effect, which was heightened only by the fact that Molière did actually meet his end as he played the part.

These experiments with dramatic illusion are, I think, a sign of this actor's constant preoccupation with the actor's chief problem, that of communication across the footlights. Molière seems to have been anxious to come out of the play to meet the audience, and in one noteworthy case he has brought the audience into the play, a signi-ficant return to medieval practice. Harpagon, seeking for the thief, determines to scrutinize everyone he meets and realizes that there is a mass of people in front of him.

'Que de gens assemblés. Je ne jette mes regards sur personne qui ne me donne des soupçons, et tout me semble mon voleur. Eh, de quoi est-ce qu'on parle là? De celui qui m'a dérobé? Quel bruit fait-on là-haut? Est-ce mon voleur qui y est? De grâce, si l'on sait des nouvelles de mon voleur, je supplie que l'on m'en dise. N'est-il point caché là parmi vous? Ils me regardent tous et se mettent à rire.'

It is hard to recollect another case in modern drama where the audience is not only given a part but where their emotional reaction is mentioned, and reckoned upon, in the text. Such realism needs the great actor to give it full scope. Here is Charles Dullin's picture of what happens: 'Il s'arrête en voyant tous les yeux des spectateurs fixés sur lui . . . il s'avance jusqu'à la rampe, il s'adresse à la dernière galerie . . . il s'agenouille et supplie. A ce moment on rit de lui. Il se relève et crie ses menaces; la passion lui ôte toute mesure.'[1]

[1] *L'Avare*, Éditions du Seuil, p. 145.

This actor was an actor-manager. His plays had to be compounded of such acting material as lay to his hand. The condition of repertory is the limited number of actors available. Is it any wonder that he suited the parts to what they could play, that he used even their physical characteristics in his (always hasty) dramatic composition? He gave Harpagon his own cough and mentioned La Flèche's limp. The chief ladies' roles were written no doubt with his talented young wife in mind; they have her artless grace and ease and charm. As an actress has said: 'En déshabillant les coquettes de Molière, nous retrouvons toujours la même Armande.' They acted together. In the *Impromptu* he says to her with a rudeness that must in a seventeenth-century theatre have seemed refreshingly natural: 'Taisez-vous, ma femme, vous êtes une bête.'

Were his more serious speeches addressed to her likewise? We here touch upon the sorest point in Molière criticism. There is evidence that they did not get on, gossip was busy with her affairs, and for a time they lived separately. When, therefore, Alceste (the man who can never conceal his feelings) cries out: 'C'est pour mes péchés que je vous aime', is it not Molière who speaks through him? To what extent this was so, no one will ever know. There is, however, all the difference between using a role for personal confession and using an actual situation as starting-point for a role. Molière's only public reference to his private affairs amounts to no more than a request that his enemies should leave them alone. Anything in the nature of subjective romantic confession is quite unthinkable from such a man, working in such a milieu, at such a trade.

Provided that we do not commit the anachronism that Musset's description of Molière suggests, we are free to think that such a play as *L'École des Femmes*, for example, owes something to the circumstances of Molière's company in 1661. It was his first full-length Paris comedy, his first attempt to fuse elegant comedy with the farce in which he felt at home; it turned out to be an unexpected success and a turning-point in his career. Having to find a role for

himself and the young wife whom he had just married, can we not
imagine him reading Scarron's story of 'La Précaution Inutile' and
thinking that the two of them might 'make something of that situation'? As he was considerably older than Armande, why not adapt
the traditional comic role of the elderly husband? It is surely legitimate to assume that, encouraged by the success of 1662, he should
write for himself and Armande such twin roles as Orgon and
Elmire, and Alceste and Célimène. If his writing were subjective
these pairs of characters would not differ greatly. But Orgon is as
different from Alceste as he is from Arnolphe. The one common
feature is the opposition of a middle-aged (choleric?) man and a
pretty 'ingénue'.

As a final piece of evidence for the influence of the actor in
Molière's comedy we should perhaps note the number of his characters who are themselves made to act. This is a feature of his play-
making, and will as such be considered in its place, but this inventor
of parts was inventing them even within the plays and scenes that he
had invented. Apparently not satisfied with a man playing a part,
Molière's dramatic instinct (or acting mania, some would say) makes
that man pretend to be even other than what he is as an actor pretending to be. This is what one scholar has aptly termed 'le démon
du théâtre'.[1] It may well be one facet of that itch for drama, for
play-acting, that accounts for the extraordinary animation of all
Molière's scenes. This implies, as his dramas show, an acute sense
of the reverse, of the process of unmasking, of causing the mask to
fall. Nor is this to be thought an idiosyncrasy of the poet Molière;
it is a thread that runs through the society that was all round him
and that supported his plays. Could he put any better mirror up to
that society than that of the mask? Were they not all compelled by
etiquette to assume the mask, to act a part, to keep up their social

---

[1] Vedel, op. cit., p. 484: 'Jouer de la comédie dans la comédie, jouer un
personnage qui à son tour en joue un autre, voilà, certes, de quoi satisfaire en
Molière le démon du théâtre.'

role? Does not all society imply the mask in its constraint upon
natural impulse? Can one ever, to other people, speak one's full
mind? What is politeness but a cloak, a mask, thrown over self-
interest? All this was tirelessly driven home by Molière's great contemporary, La Rochefoucauld, for whom 'le monde n'est composé
que de mines'.[1] It may be no accident that in a whole group of his
Maximes the Duke refers expressly to actors as presenting a type
and figure of all social behaviour.

But here we come upon the difference between Molière and his
dramatic teachers. In their hands the mask is fixed, so that the character affixed to the player may be recognized. For Molière, impressed
as he was with the affixed character, it is only affixed, and to a living
organism. The point of interest for him, and for us, is the point
when the mask slips or falls, when the underlying man appears.
This distinction is never absent from Molière's plays. All his situations gravitate to that moment when the mask is removed; he steers
them towards this abandonment of the mask and consequent emer-
gence of the natural. We must now inquire how far this is a principle on which his plays are actually built.

[1] *Maximes*, 256.

III. MASK

IT was the purpose of the last chapter to suggest that many features of Molière's comedy are to be explained by his profession, that his plays should be read as the work of a man who was not primarily satirist or moralist but an actor, a 'comédien'. The peculiar feature and symbol of the dramatic tradition in which he was trained was the mask, and something has been said of the way in which Molière renewed this symbol. But the argument has now to be taken a stage further. Assuming for a moment that his plays show cases of social habit as a kind of mask covering human nature, should one say more than this? What is the connexion between Molière's skill in portraying assumed attitudes (masks) and the comic vision that is the dynamic and formative element of his work? In other words, has the mask anything to do with the principle of comedy as Molière imagined it? The question might be settled without difficulty if we were agreed what that principle is, but since it is the purpose of these chapters to inquire what it is, we must proceed from the mask to the comedy rather than fit the mask to a presupposition of the comedy.[1]

It is obvious, to begin with, that many comic effects can be obtained by the juxtaposition of the real and the assumed. This is

[1] Part of this chapter has appeared in the *Modern Language Review*, xliii. 1.

a frequent source of comedy in ordinary life and one would not expect a trained comedian, whose business it was to distil comedy from any kind of situation, to pass it by. What the valet really thinks of his master is of course very different from what he can say in his presence. The comic dramatist arranges a situation in which the two views clash and amuse by the abruptness of the contrast. Thus Sganarelle:

'Mon maître est un fourbe, il n'a dessein que de vous abuser, et en a bien abusé d'autres, c'est l'épouseur du genre humain, et . . . (apercevant Don Juan) Cela est faux; et quiconque vous dira cela, vous lui devez dire qu'il en a menti. Mon maître n'est point l'épouseur du genre humain, il n'est point un fourbe, il n'a pas dessein de vous tromper, et n'en a point abusé d'autres. Ah, tenez, le voilà; demandez-le plutôt à lui-même.'

The valet may be released from his mask of discretion not by the absence of his master, but by freedom to speak his mind. Harpagon is curious to know what people think of him, and Maître Jacques reluctantly consents to tell him, only to be beaten and told to 'learn how to speak'. It is amusing, and liberating, to see the mask of convention removed, because in real life this rarely happens.

But discretion imposed by social status is a simple form of mask. What of that imposed by one's views, attitude, temperament? We meet many people whose behaviour is dictated by an idea, a way of looking at things. The seventeenth century called this 'imagination' and saw in it, in Pascal's words, an enemy of reason, which it dominates and subdues, to the extent of establishing within man 'a second nature'. On this point Pascal and Molière seem to be in almost verbal agreement. One might imagine Pascal's notes written down with some of the comedies in mind. 'L'imagination', he says, 'a ses heureux, ses malheureux, ses sains, ses malades, ses riches, ses pauvres . . . elle a ses fous et ses sages. . . . Combien de malades lui sont redevables de leur santé et combien de sains de leur maladie . . . richesses inutiles à celui qui s'imagine n'en avoir pas assez . . . .'

Molière has animated for us these people who get things wrong and who live in a world of their own, the hypochondriac, for example, or the miser. Even his titles emphasize their delusion: *Le Cocu Imaginaire, Le Malade Imaginaire.* Is not Jourdain of this family also, the bourgeois who apes the gentry, who imagines himself a man of quality? And in such plays we are given hints of a real man other than the mask of his delusion. Argan thinks he is ill and weak because he believes his doctors, but when he forgets what they say he is strong and shows that he can do what he will never admit he can do. Harpagon is at times an inhuman miser with no thought for people, at others a human being sensitive to lack of affection.

These are cases of human nature covered by a mask which is unconscious. But we meet yet another category, whose policy it is to play a part, rogues, schemers, charlatans. The doctors do not get things wrong; they lead others wrong; they are not deceived but deceivers. They assume a mask of omniscience for their own profit. Arnolphe is a tyrant, Tartuffe a hypocrite, Don Juan a libertine, each for his own ends. But here surely the simile of the mask breaks down; in these cases is not the mask the man? Yet here again they have other qualities which they are anxious to hide, which are not assumed but almost completely suppressed. Arnolphe is timid, Tartuffe sensual, Don Juan is warm-hearted as well as calculating. They are clever, but not clever enough to take us in all the time. Is not their cleverness a mask, the more dramatic for being imposed by their own will? If this is so, Molière has turned the mask into a symbol of much more than a vice or defect that adheres to a man. It is a symbol of cleverness, art, skill on which a man prides himself, but which may well run counter to his real self. The struggle to keep the mask in place, to achieve one's end, becomes a struggle between art and nature, craft and habit, intelligence and character. If such be Molière's principle of comedy, is it not nearer poetry than realism?

These points may be tested by scrutiny of such a play as *L'École des Femmes.* Arnolphe is a man with a plan of which he is proud, and which is inhuman to the point of involving the stultification of a human being. He speaks of his ward, to whom his plan has denied a proper education, in the most impersonal and callous terms. He has indeed all the marks of the crank, filled with the persuasion that he is right, that no one can teach him anything, that by his ingenuity he has solved a problem that has perplexed the world for centuries. The plan is, in a word, the School for Wives. It sets out to ensure fidelity in the wife by making her unattractive and completely dependent upon her husband. Furthermore, Arnolphe has not only skill and confidence; he has luck; he holds all the cards and is even informed by his opponent of each step taken or contemplated by the other side. Nevertheless his plan fails. Why? Many reasons might be given. No doubt because things are so arranged that the other side (whom we as spectators want to see victorious) are allowed, for our pleasure, to be so. But why do we sympathize with them, or rather, why has the dramatist so put the position that we all do want Arnolphe to be defeated? We might say that we 'naturally' side against him. He is trying to interfere with nature, and nature defeats him. The famous letter written by Agnès is a poignant document: 'Comme je commence à croire qu'on m'a toujours tenue dans l'ignorance, j'ai peur de mettre quelquechose qui ne soit pas bien.' Who can read this powerful description of an awakening natural faculty without sympathy? The struggle within and behind the play is one between artifice and nature.

But what happens to Arnolphe? He is beaten, but does he admit his error, and reform, or think out a better plan? Some contemporaries were scandalized at the end of the play, and denied that he was a comic figure at all. To leave him tricked and cheated, even though he deserved to lose, what is comic about this? The answer is, nothing. The comedy of the play does not consist wholly, or even chiefly, in the fact that nature has been lucky enough to outwit art. That would come to little more than *Schadenfreude.* There is another Arnolphe than the crank. The crank is inhuman, but Arnolphe falls in love; in no grand way, certainly; it is a kind of sensual calf-love, but it is no part of his plan; it is a feeling quite opposed to the plan and which he obviously had not reckoned upon at all. When he is in power he says, parodying the heroes of Corneille,

> Je suis maître, je parle; allez, obéissez,

as one might talk to a dog. This is the tone of the Maxims of Marriage which he pontifically makes Agnès read in order that she may fully realize her wifely duty. Yet in a later scene we find him on his knees professing that he will do anything for her, that she need make no promises, nor even be faithful:

> Tout comme tu voudras tu pourras te conduire.

The mask is off. The man who was going to prove that a woman could be made so unattractive that no one would entice her away from her husband has fallen for the creature he tried to stultify. Instead of a confident tyrant we see a grovelling silly lover, and see him with pleasure, not because we rejoice that his scheme has come to nothing, for perhaps we never took it seriously, but because we have been led to glimpse the reality beneath the mask. This is not pretty, but it is at least real, and human, and unpretentious.

The play has been called a study of jealousy and I cannot think the claim will be taken seriously. These impossible and farcical situations would invalidate any serious study of jealousy. Beside *Othello* this play would seem a bungler's work. But as a comedy, constantly opposing the natural to the assumed and unnatural, the play is alive, no bungling but an admirably graded sequence of conflicts, leaving a single aesthetic impression. With its aesthetic we are not for the moment concerned, but with the principle of the mask that lies near its centre.

A similar vision of normality, disturbed by the cunning of an impostor, is found in a greater and more famous comedy, *Tartuffe*.

It is remarkable that for many people this great play has ceased to be a comedy at all; it is often read as if it were a realistic satire. No one could deny that sinister forces are here suggested in powerful fashion. The mask of hypocrisy is an almost perfect fit, and ensures a steady increase of power to the wearer. It is probable that in a first three-act version of the play the mask was never removed and was completely successful. But that hypocrisy is a mask there should be no doubt. The sub-title of *L'Imposteur* settles the question. The play is about a man who gives himself out to be what he is not; he wears the mask of piety and that is not in itself a comic proceeding, unless or until it be shown to be . . . a mask, and not the man.

This elementary contrast within the man who plays a part is surely a basic feature of the role of Tartuffe. The part he plays is of vital importance to him. It assures his well-being and his domination over his fellows. It is the mask of a pious attitude, ascetic, world-renouncing, sanctimonious: 'Couvrez ce sein que je ne saurais voir' (860). But this part is not kept up all the time. We see more than the mask, at times, when for one reason or another he is not hypo-critical but sincere. In any judgement of the part it would seem vital to ask when the mask falls. Can anything be deduced from the alternation of hypocrisy and sincerity? In the case of a classical dramatist this may reveal the dramatic purpose. The mask falls at four points of the action, twice with Orgon and twice with Elmire. Nowhere else in the play, as far as I can see, does Tartuffe pretend to be other than a holy man. These four points of the action are worth close scrutiny.

The first is the famous third scene of the third act. 'Mon sein n'enferme pas un cœur qui soit de pierre' (930); with this statement the hypocrite seems to me to be leaving his role. It is the first of a series of ambiguous statements, which are true of his real nature as well as of the mask he has assumed. The point is more evident when he says: 'Ah, pour être dévot je n'en suis pas moins homme.' He intends surely to convey by this that humanity is not incompatible with piety. But his statement is true of himself as a natural and evil man: that his piety has not (in the least) affected his humanity, a statement which as a lover he may sustain, but which as an ascetic he would not. The same double echo is heard in a moment: 'Mais Madame, après tout, je ne suis pas un ange' (970). From this Tartuffe proceeds to something which is not ambiguous at all, to an avowal of sharp practice and trickery which he would not for the world have anyone but Elmire overhear:

> Mais les gens comme nous brûlent d'un feu discret
> Avec qui pour toujours on est sûr du secret. . . .
> Et c'est en nous qu'on trouve, acceptant notre cœur,
> De l'amour sans scandale et du plaisir sans peur. (995.)

This is the complete avowal, by the *masqué*, that his mask is a mask. It may not be funny; it is deeply comic.

The second glimpse of Tartuffe's sincerity seems to me even more instructive for the aesthetics of this play. Three scenes later (III. vi) Tartuffe, accused of seducing his employer's wife, pleads guilty, as indeed he was. His statements are all true:

> Chaque instant de ma vie est chargé de souillures. . . .
> Vous fiez-vous, mon frère, à mon extérieur?
> Et, pour tout ce qu'on voit, me croyez-vous meilleur?
> Non, non. Vous vous laissez tromper à l'apparence,
> Et je ne suis rien moins, hélas, que ce qu'on pense.
> Tout le monde me prend pour un homme de bien;
> Mais la vérité pure est que je ne vaux rien. (1077, 1095–1100.)

How can one escape the comedy of hearing, from one whose profession and practice it was to disguise the truth, 'la vérité pure'? With extreme ingenuity Molière forces his impostor into a second situation where he can drop the mask, a situation quite different from the first. For here to tell the truth is not the result of natural, animal desire; it is the fruit of policy. To tell the truth in that context is the highest and most successful deception. He is not believed.

So he can assume the mask once more and cover his own advantage with the will of heaven:

> La volonté du Ciel soit faite en toute chose. (1181)

It is, I suppose, highly unlikely that the first version of the play contained a second interview between Tartuffe and Elmire. There must have been strong reasons for making the impostor walk a second time into an obvious trap. Before we assume a weakness on the part of the dramatist let us note what is gained by the repetition. The force of the satire is not increased. The character of Orgon is not affected. But the impostor is this time not only completely exposed by his words, but actually discovered beyond hope of justification. The mask is, so to speak, almost torn off his face. To the objection that a clever scoundrel would have foreseen and avoided a second encounter there is a plain answer. That Tartuffe does not foresee it is a feature of his character; it is the final proof that he was not in that connexion wise, cautious, or cunning any longer; that, in a word, he was infatuated. Once again the impostor is sincere, sincere in his hesitation, in his professions of pleasure at her words which he longs to hear:

> Leur miel dans tous mes sens fait couler à longs traits
> Une suavité qu'on ne goûta jamais. (1439)

Sincere also in his application to her of religious terms describing the happiness he may never have really felt before God but does actually feel before her, and sincere above all in his gross sensuality, that demands more than words, what she calls 'les dernières faveurs' and he 'des réalités'. This is the real world in which he moves, and having admitted it he scoffs at morality:

> Si ce n'est que le Ciel qu'à mes vœux on oppose,
> Lever un tel obstacle est pour moi peu de chose.

To fear God is a ridiculous fear (1485); casuistry can cover anything. Sin does not count when concealed: 'Ce n'est pas pécher que pécher en silence.' The new morality is to follow one's director blindly:

> Vous n'avez seulement qu'à vous laisser conduire. (1494)

In the following scene there is a final glimpse of the real man. When his pious excuses are cut short he claims that he is master of the house, in the eyes of the law, that he will be a match for all of them, and thus (picking up the mask again) avenge heaven (1562). In his last scene the mask is slightly adjusted to that of the good citizen. He regards as his first duty the good of the State (1880). It is of some aesthetic importance to note that he ends, as he began, by provoking Dorine's pungent comment, 'L'imposteur' (1885).

If the foregoing analysis be sound, we are faced in this play with a character at once more profound and more comic than has been made clear. There is, to begin with, no doubt of its realism. The author himself had in a significant stage-direction (to line 1487) to call attention to the fact that his impostor was a scoundrel. He is indeed a sinister figure, 'escroc cherché par la police' as Vedel says, whom we fear rather than laugh at. Brunetière expressed the typical reaction of the intelligent spectator: 'Si nous rions à ses déconvenues, il n'en reste pas moins un fourbe renommé dont nous avons au total plus de peur que d'envie de rire, et si l'on veut qu'il soit comique il l'est sans doute, messieurs, mais d'une façon qui n'appartient qu'à lui.'[1] What for Brunetière was a grudging admission is roundly denied by Michaut, as by so many readers. He admits that but for a single passage he does not find Tartuffe comic at all. Agreed, if comedy be limited to the pleasant things on the surface of life, if 'comic' be more or less equated with 'funny' and thus barred from dealing with mystery and evil. But there is no evidence that Molière held this view, nor that the wiser of his contemporaries thought his play less profound than the tragedies of Racine.

The view that *Tartuffe* is a comedy does not imply any softening of the character of the impostor. We may admit him to be a sinister figure, but we should at the same time notice that Molière has stressed this aspect far less than others. As a dangerous man he is kept in the background and hardly ever seen at work. As a contrast

[1] *Époques du théâtre français*, p. 138.

in and to himself he is exhibited in an endless variety of pose. Molière was apparently not satisfied with the contrast in the nature of an impostor, that his acts are at variance with his professions. He carries the contrast to a much deeper level, to situations which force the impostor to be himself, to drop the mask, as we have shown. It is vital to notice how close is the connexion between Tartuffe's sincerity and his undoing. He is unmasked, not primarily by others, not by Damis, or the police, but (in our eyes, and it is after all for the audience that the dramatic spectacle is staged) by himself. More than this, he is not unmasked by his slips, or by a faulty technique, but because, and whenever, he wants to be. His scheme, in fact, of being an impostor will not work. At times he does not want it to work. Where intellectual ends are involved it works to perfection; where more elementary and more human ends are involved, such as the satisfaction of his animal desires, the scheme does not work at all; it breaks down, because he is too human to allow it to work. Brunetière has seen something of the connexion between his skill and his weakness: 'Chaque tentative que l'on fait pour le démasquer ou pour le déloger ne réussit qu'à l'ancrer davantage, plus profondément et plus solidement dans l'affection d'Orgon. Aussi n'en sortirions nous pas, s'il n'avait heureusement un point faible — c'est sa sensualité.'[1] But why should this cardinal point be ascribed to luck? Nothing is lucky in classical drama; all is design. Tartuffe fails, as M. Michaut has made clear, precisely because he was overconfident of his powers, because he reckoned without his appetites. 'Son malheur est que le succès l'a grisé; il a trop confiance en son pouvoir de séduction. Sa sensualité, qu'il ne surveille pas, l'aveugle; il se déclare ... il tombe dans le piège ... scélérat étonnant de vérité dans le conflit même de ses diverses passions.'[2] It is not far from such a conception to discovery of the comic principle lying at the root of such a character. Is it so much a 'malheur' that Tartuffe's

[1] Op. cit., p. 125.
[2] *Les Luttes de Molière*, p. 131.

human nature escapes his calculation? Is this not the real nerve of
the play?

A third example should stand beside the two already analysed if
the evidence is to have its full weight. But the character and situation of Alceste need not be described at length as the relevant points
can be briefly made clear. The subject of the play, as its latest editor
has remarked, is comparable to that of *Tartuffe*: 'l'hypocrisie reli-
gieuse conduit tout droit à l'hypocrisie sociale.'[1] There are many
things in *Le Misanthrope* beside any symbolism of the mask, but it
is noteworthy that this man who claims to base his case upon reason,
who in his assertions of principle is a tiresome doctrinaire, is not
only unreasonable but bad-tempered, selfish, brusque. He is, in fact,
very far from the man he thinks he is or that he blames others for not
being. His views, his doctrine, are in sharp contrast to his nature,
his mood, his real situation. The contrast is pointed by his engage-
ment to a lady of whose views he is most critical. He admits that she
is not his type:

> Il est vrai, ma raison me le dit chaque jour;
> Mais la raison n'est pas ce qui règle l'amour. (247)

Tartuffe, one remembers, made much the same admission:

> Un cœur se laisse prendre et ne raisonne pas. (968)

This parallel is not fortuitous. The role of love in these comedies
is so similar as to warrant our close attention. Each of three main
characters is betrayed, as he would call it, by the same agency. His
plan is ruined by the fact of his falling in love. It is curious not only
that their roles should have much in common but that the agency of
their failure should be the same. A comic trick? No doubt, and one
that Molière had seen and had used before. In the old farce one
would laugh with the lovers against the pedants or tyrannical
guardians. But the proceeding here gathers (as do so many others in
Molière's work) its full sense and power by being perfectly moti-

[1] *Le Misanthrope*, ed. Rudler, p. v.

vated. The motivation is not very hard to discover. Is not love a symbol for what is not the mask but the man, for nature, as opposed to art? It is contrary to idea and policy; it is unpremeditated and even in a sense unwelcome. The lover curses his luck that he should be in love. But it is beyond human power to control; it is an instinct, not an idea.

Comedy founded on this antagonism of the wits and the instinct is deeply founded in human nature. For normal human nature includes both the feelings and the ideas, brain and heart, reason and instinct. Molière presumed in his audience a normal balance of the two elements. But the deceiver, or the fool, or the doctrinaire prides himself on his wits, his ideas, his reason. He leaves his instinct out of the reckoning; he adopts a mask of intelligence. But instinct will be revenged and returns unexpectedly; the mask has to fall.

Such a view of human nature is, as one would expect from a 'comédien', different from both the Christian and the rationalist interpretations current in Molière's day. It agrees with the Christian psychology of Pascal, who said 'nous sommes automate autant qu'esprit', that rationalism is a simplification. But to many Christians it would seem pagan in its assumption of normality and balance. It might seem inspired by that humanism of the Renaissance which regarded all the instincts as right. This is why Molière was regarded as a libertin, 'peut-être le seul agressif' said Perrens. The difficulty is that in the plays no conclusions are drawn; a picture is presented. The picture seems to me to fit neither the Christianity of Bossuet nor the worship of nature, which for Brunetière was Molière's philosophy. It is a picture of contrast within the autonomous personality. The power of will and of wit is checked by what most people think the inferior power of instinct and sense. Men are shown as inhuman in their worship of power and intellect; they are human only in their baser instincts. But for his gross sensuality Tartuffe would be a robot. What Christians call our lower nature is seen as saving our superior qualities. But perhaps we should not be too easily alarmed. All depends on what conclusions are drawn. Molière is doing no more than present a picture of normality. And it agrees with that suggested by some of his great contemporaries. It is expressed indeed in the aphorism of Pascal: 'La nature soutient la raison impuissante et l'empêche d'extravaguer à ce point.' Molière might reply that his picture showed up the illusion of Renaissance man that he could order his own existence. The pride of the over-clever and the over-confident is severely handled in his drama, as in that of Racine. But his vision of normality includes instinct as a corrective. Did La Rochefoucauld not admit as much when he wrote that 'l'homme croit souvent se conduire lorsqu'il est conduit'?

IV. SPEECH

I⟨T⟩ is some years since M. Faguet pointed out that the French classical dramatists obtained their effects by means much more restricted than those at the disposal of either the Greeks or the Elizabethans. Neither music nor religious ceremony as in Greek drama, neither physical nor topographical features as in the Elizabethan; for the French the sole and entire vehicle of dramatic action is the spoken word. If this be true, the principles and the symbolism that lie behind the language of classical drama are in need of further investigation. When, for example, we listen to Phèdre saying

> J'ai dit ce que jamais on ne devait entendre

we may not be conscious that the poet suggests a divorce between actual speech (what she has said) and a speech convention (what it was possible, socially, to say). This distinction could hardly be overstepped in the society for which *Phèdre* was written; dramatic intensity has therefore carried the character beyond what in the real world was permitted. The aesthetic effect of such a spectacle might be worth investigation.

The comic dramatist had this advantage over the tragedian that he was allowed to use ordinary speech and gesture, and not trammelled by the tradition of stilted declamation against which Molière rebelled even in tragedy. Furthermore, the *farceur* had the additional resource of dumb show and mime. Molière's acting was not confined to what he said. 'Ses grimaces, son corps de caoutchouc, son bagou, étaient selon ses ennemis un peu trop d'un pitre.'[1] What he himself referred to as 'tout le jeu du théâtre' must have been a singularly close alliance of word and gesture; traces of the original vivacity still cling to the printed text, and actors have been said to find Molière's parts naturally suited to the gestures implied in the words.

Molière's career as a maker of comedy shows a fascinating development in the use and handling of language. As we have seen, he was trained by actors who attached relatively little importance to set words; the roles in the *commedia dell' arte* were not even written down, and were left for the actor to improvise under the inspiration of actual impersonation. This, were it still available, might give us the most living and 'dramatic' form of diction possible, the words being entirely subservient to the mime. Compared with it classical comedy is a deformation to the point of being a contradiction in terms, for the diction of comedy, traditionally, was that of homely and everyday speech; that of the five-act play in verse was almost the reverse, artificial, conventional, obeying laws of euphony and style rather than of life and instinct. How Molière fused these two kinds of diction is an unexplained marvel. Yet the thing was done and can still be admired in the text of his more serious plays. Only the fantasy of genius could produce the delightful ambivalence of *Le Misanthrope*, where figurative and abstract expressions abound:

> Certes, pour un amant la fleurette est mignonne (509);

where the lines can be as flat as any ordinary statement:

> Si vous faites cela, vous ne ferez pas peu (235);

and can even show the gaucherie of a clumsy doctrinaire:

> Nous verrons si c'est moi que vous voudrez qui sorte. (742)

Apart from this fusion of style and nature there would seem to be

[1] Vedel, op. cit., p. 464.

little cause to examine the kinds of diction in Molière, so obviously and completely does he seem to have fitted speech to the expression of ordinary people in undignified situations. It would be, therefore, out of place to seek in his work for evidence of a poetic renewal of language such as we find in Shakespeare. Yet just as his work contains more than realism, so its diction is not at all points parallel with that of living people; it gives more enjoyment, its features are more pronounced; it has balance and symmetry. It is in fact an artistic counterpart to ordinary speech, as life in the comedies is an artistic counterpart to ordinary existence.

Just as we do not find in this diction any considerable trace of a formative or poetic use of words, in the manner of Rabelais or Shakespeare, so we look in vain for the polish and wit of Restoration comedy. Witticisms, puns, quips, these occur but not very frequently, and often in very elementary form. Sganarelle infuriates his wife, when she complains that she is left with 'quatre pauvres petits enfants sur les bras', with the laconic rejoinder: 'Mets-les à terre.' Accused of eating up her substance he corrects the reproach to 'drinking up part of it'. Wit of a neater kind is found, in *Amphitryon*, for example, when Mercury remarks of Jupiter's conduct, 'c'est agir en dieu qui n'est pas bête', and that 'les bêtes ne sont pas si bêtes que l'on pense'. It is perhaps a pointer that the memorable sayings in Molière, those that have caught popular imagination and passed into proverb or cliché, these are not witty sayings in the ordinary sense. 'Il vaut mieux être marié que mort', 'nous avons changé tout cela', these have more of the epigram about them than the witticism; they seem to condense a volume of rough sense or naïve rascality into a phrase. They suggest a technique almost the reverse of rabelaisian; there is here no effort to extend or strain ordinary usage, but to stuff into an everyday frame an unusual amount of life or vigour.

Analysis of Molière's diction confirms this hint. Its chief characteristics are vigour and vivacity; it has the dramatic quality *par*

excellence, the quality of compressed and explosive life; it is sometimes ungrammatical and the more vibrant for that. 'Rends-le moi
sans te fouiller', says Harpagon. The point has been well put
already:

'Comme sous l'effet d'un vin pétillant, le sang circule plus vite, les
idées, les mots jaillissent plus facilement que chez nous autres, la vie est
plus intense, l'ensemble du jeu plus animé au delà de la rampe que de
notre côté. . . . Toutes choses qu'on évite dans un texte élaboré à la
table de travail, mais qui donnent à la langue parlée fraîcheur et vie, font
assister le spectateur à la naissance des idées du personnage, à son travail
pour les exprimer, les démêler les unes des autres, les ranger: reprises,
amendements, impatientes abréviations et ellipses, répétitions, sauts,
maladresses.'[1]

The critic here cited goes on to show how the same characteristic
animates the characters, and is the sign of Molière's general presentation of life and action, compressed vigour, heightened liveliness.
This is what we should expect from a *farceur* of genius. This indeed
was the aim of farce: to shock and fascinate by the illusion of life, to
be alive, at the cost of crudity, indecency, unreality, improbability.
The strain runs, refined and purified, through Molière's whole work.
It is one of the great laws of drama (and one that the farce of his day
exemplified better than any contemporary form of play) that life on
the stage must be abbreviated, curtailed, selected, and the loss in
continuity and variety made up in concision, artificial variety, life,
energy. The feature common to high farce like *Le Médecin malgré
lui* and the profound comedy of *L'Avare* is perhaps just this irre-
pressible life and resource. No rest, no quiet moments, something
new, alive, unexpected all the time; Harpagon storms through the
play as restlessly as Sganarelle twists and turns through his irre-
sistible attitudes. To quote Vedel once more: 'Les marquis sots et
frétillants comme leurs coquins de valets ont du vif-argent dans les
veines.'

The consequences of this for the language of the plays are more

[1] Vedel, op. cit., p. 465.

simple and suggestive than might be supposed. Whereas psychology, character-drawing, and satire might lead to an intellectual use of language, to precision, distinction, and differentiation, the concentration of dramatic energy in person and situation leads to the opposite. Excitability of any kind, be it irritation, mania, gaiety, anger, or fun, leads to incoherence, which is that state in which one's power of intelligent expression in words is defeated. Language in Molière shows with almost infinite variety this clash of man and speech. The gift of speech is the mark of the intelligent or civilized man; natural man, animal man is frequently speechless. He might, if he could, say with Dandin: 'Je ne dis mot, car je ne gagnerais rien à parler.' Or even more frequently his utterance escapes his control: he says what he does not mean, or less, or more, than he means. Here for a dramatist dealing chiefly in words was a wide field of evidence of human behaviour under the pressure of emotion. Molière has, as I hope to show, exploited it as no other artist has done.

To do this at all implies a firm understanding of the social function of language. At its simplest, language is communication and in normal intercourse language obeys the single condition that both parties understand what is said. Samuel Butler had it that the essential ingredients of language were three: a sayer, a sayee, and a convention. Someone must speak, someone must hear, both must understand more or less the same thing by what is said: what the one emits the other must admit. When this is not so, language fails in its social function; it is, we say, unintelligible, it is misunderstood, or in more pictorial explanatory phrase, it does not get across. Many rudimentary comic situations are no more than interferences with this structure of three-point relationship. Suppose, for instance, that the speaker is not sure who is at the other end of the chain of communication, or that he thinks the hearer is someone other than he really is. Suppose again that what he says is not heard, or not grasped, or misinterpreted. These elementary cases occur in Molière. Horace betrays the whole story to Arnolphe because he mistakes his identity. But what would in real life give rise to an amusing remark or incident is screwed up, so to speak, by the dramatist in order to produce its maximum comic potential. The situation is arranged so that Horace does not merely give the show away, but relates to Arnolphe, as if he were a third party, the discomfiture of Arnolphe, and not only so but expects Arnolphe to be as amused as he is, and comments on the fact that he is not laughing enough. The mock soldier in the *Fourberies* asks Argante if he has seen 'ce faquin d'Argante' and describes in blood-curdling terms (to Argante) what he would do to him if he should happen to find him. The effect is due to nothing more than mistaken identity and consequently misdirected language. Its more philosophic development will be noticed later.

A similar everyday case is that of being misheard. Of this, too, there are cases in Molière, but intensified again to a degree that rarely occurs in life. La Flèche (deliberately?) mishears the most suspicious of men, thus: Harpagon: 'Ne serais-tu point un homme à faire courir le bruit que j'ai chez moi de l'argent caché? — Vous avez de l'argent caché? — Non, coquin, je ne dis pas cela.' A variant of this is Sganarelle's (deliberate?) misunderstanding of the doctors' verdict on his daughter: 'Nous avons vu suffisamment la malade et sans doute qu'il y a beaucoup d'impuretés en elle. — Ma fille est impure?'

One of the basic assumptions and intentions of social speech is its comprehensibility: it conveys the mind and intention of the speaker. Speech that does not do this is comic; we laugh, for example, at a man who speaks and yet has nothing to say. But such a man is not often so funny as Molière makes Sganarelle. As a doctor, called to pronounce on a case, he cannot appear tongue-tied, he has nothing relevant to say; his speech, therefore, is nonsense, clothed in the forms of sense: 'Hippocrate dit . . . que nous nous couvrions tous deux. — Hippocrate dit cela? — Oui. — Dans quel chapitre, s'il vous plaît? — Dans son chapitre . . . des chapeaux.'

A parallel case is incoherence, that of a man who has something in his mind but cannot express it. The seventeenth century admitted that language did not suffice to express all that men wished to express. The quality too rare or precious to admit of precise definition was known as 'je ne sais quoi', which is possibly one of the many *précieux* expressions which have justified their invention. But Molière is alive to the comedy of the position of having to define the indefinable. Alceste, when asked what is wrong with him, cannot, for excellent reasons, say what it is: 'J'ai ce que sans mourir je ne puis concevoir.' It is perhaps fitting that a Frenchman should have given such delightful expression to this incapacity to express. The most dramatic case occurs in *Tartuffe*. Orgon, attempting to describe Tartuffe, cannot find words to do so:

C'est un homme ... qui ... ah ... un homme ... un homme enfin ... .,

a line which appears to mirror exactly the stuttering of a man who has the will, but not the capacity, to speak, but which is fuller, rounder, more intense than life, since it embodies a triple statement: that Orgon cannot describe him, that he is indescribable (which is true, but in a different sense for Orgon and for us), and finally that any attempt to describe him can only say that he is ... a man, which in fact he hardly is. For Orgon he is almost the perfect man; for the others he is almost inhuman. Thus can language, under a guise of helpless incoherence, unite in a single expression allusion to widely differing states of mind.

What might be called a complementary phenomenon is even more impressive. A man may be incoherent because he has too much in his mind to say. The artistic parallel to this is speech, in a moment of intensity, that says far more than is meant. Again, the logical function of speech is broken, we should perhaps say broken through, by nature, by emotion that ruins the intended effect of speech and conveys not the meaning of the speaker but his real state, possibly against his will. The language of Molière's maniacs and fools is no longer the vehicle of their intention, but conveys in its sweep and force their condition also. Argan, for example, at the end of a long duel of repartee admits, as he never would wittingly do, his own evil nature. (The situation had been already worked out in similar fashion in the *Fourberies*.)

'Voici qui est plaisant. Je ne mettrai pas ma fille dans un couvent si je veux ? — Non, vous dis-je. — Qui m'en empêchera ? — Vous-même. — Moi ? — Oui. Vous n'aurez pas ce cœur-là. — Je l'aurai. — Vous vous moquez. — Je ne me moque point. — La tendresse paternelle vous prendra. — Elle ne me prendra point. — Une petite larme ou deux, des bras jetés au cou, un mon petit papa mignon, prononcé tendrement, sera assez pour vous toucher. — Tout cela ne fera rien. — Oui, oui. — Je vous dis que je n'en démordrai point — Bagatelles. — Il ne faut point dire : Bagatelles. — Mon Dieu, je vous connais, vous êtes bon naturelle-ment. — Je ne suis point bon, je suis méchant quand je veux.'

The same kind of situation occurs in *Tartuffe*, showing the same pastiche of realism, but only a pastiche; surely no people ever quarrelled with this remorseless logic, getting nearer and nearer to the absurd as they get more excited, until the wire-puller produces the final unmasking absurdity. This is no realism, but a sovereign exercise of dramatic irony. In the first love-scene the hypocrite ardently pleads his case, but at the same time provides, for those who overhear, the admission of his own rascality. The lady claims to be shocked at his 'déclaration tout-à-fait galante' coming from a man of piety, and thus provokes him to say:

Ah, pour être dévot je n'en suis pas moins homme. . . .
Je sais qu'un tel discours de moi paraît étrange
Mais, Madame, après tout, je ne suis pas un ange.

His meaning is clear, but so also is that grosser meaning that he did not intend to convey but which his words would carry to the audience. One might paraphrase his intention thus: 'My piety does not make me any less a man', which also means that his piety does not affect his humanity, because it is only skin-deep. And with the confession that he was 'no angel' would not Damis and Dorine boisterously agree, reading into it the most joyful litotes? No angel, that was a rich way to describe him.

As a variant of this dramatic trick of forcing a man to say two things when he thinks he is only saying one, the famous monologue of Harpagon shows case after case of statements pushed beyond their meaning and exaggerated to absurdity by the passion of the utterance. The equivalent in word does not seem strong enough, so the speaker embroiders on the concept and pushes it beyond the credible, thus:

> Au voleur, au voleur, à l'assassin, au meurtrier. . . . Je suis perdu, je suis assassiné, on m'a coupé la gorge. . . . C'en est fait, je n'en puis plus, je me meurs, je suis mort, je suis enterré. N'y a-t-il personne qui veuille me ressusciter en me rendant mon cher argent. . . . Je veux aller quérir la justice, et faire donner la question à toute la maison. . . . Allons vite, des commissaires, des archers, des prévôts, des juges, des gênes, des potences et des bourreaux. Je veux faire pendre tout le monde, et si je ne retrouve mon argent, je me pendrai moi-même après.

To talk like this is certainly grotesque; it is also the mark of a lunatic, but the exaggerating method is clear enough in each case for us to realize that the force behind the words is striving always to surpass them, to find the impossible, that is, words to equal his horror at the theft, a horror which is strictly and soberly speaking indescribable: it goes beyond words. But this is a feature of other 'possédés' in Molière's comedies. Alceste had perhaps no idea of how much he was giving away when he said: 'Personne n'a, Madame, aimé comme je fais', until the phrase was out and capped immediately by the cool rejoinder: 'En effet, la méthode en est toute nouvelle.'

Perhaps Orgon's famous repetitions are to be accounted for in similar fashion. Here again criticism has yielded perhaps too easily to the assumption that what is not deep and serious psychology is a blemish, a *lazzo* of farce introduced to catch the gallery or to lighten the tone. The scene is unreal, but so is all fantasy. And it is surely a plausible fantasy that the master of the house should inquire about what is going on, that the servant should speak only of Madame, about whom he can find out for himself, that he should therefore interrupt her with his 'Et Tartuffe?' and after each of her taunts against the holy man should ejaculate 'Le pauvre homme!' This is comic, not as pointless repetition but as the language of absorption. The fact that his sole reflection should fall so faultlessly in place means nothing to him and much to the audience.

Let us now see how the rogues use language to their own purposes. Language is as comic when designedly misused as when it unintentionally betrays. The source of comedy lies in the fact of interference with the normal process of communication; in the one case the man's nature or passion interferes with his intention; in the other his intention deliberately obscures or twists or abandons normal speech in order to attain a particular end. The clearest example of this procedure is professional jargon. Words are used for an effect other than that conveyed by their meaning. They convey perhaps no actual sense at all but an aura of authority. One can watch the gap widen between their meaninglessness and their effect. This makes nonsense into an effective form of language: what is without meaning can impress fools. Sganarelle, delighted that none of the company know Latin, reels off a meaningless string of words at which his audience gapes with admiration: 'Ah, que n'ai-je étudié? — L'habile homme que voilà. — Oui, ça est si biau que je n'y entends goutte.' Diafoirus finds Argan's pulse 'duriuscule pour ne pas dire dur'. He gets over a diagnosis directly opposed to that of a colleague by equating the two with a great show of authority: 'Eh oui, rôti, bouilli, même chose.' The curses of Purgon are in the same category; like much of Molière's irony, they are effective on the man who sees magic power in them; they are joyously ridiculous for the audience who see there is no meaning in them.

And there are, in the same play, superior cases of this irony. Authority is perhaps less dramatic when it replaces argument than when it confirms bad argument. Thanks to his authority, to his professional standing, to his use of the right academic jargon, and to his undoubted skill, Diafoirus is able to prove that black is white. In the very presence of his slow-witted son, described in stage directions as having 'une mine tout-à-fait niaise', he undertakes to convince Argan that the boy is a desirable marriage partner. His speech is a masterpiece of specious argument. Studiously moderate, admitting that appearances are against him, and all the while insinuating points that each tell for something against the appearances, he almost succeeds in reversing the firmest judgements of sense-impression. He admits what others might call a certain quietness, dullness, and slowness in the boy, whom none who know him would describe as given to devilry. 'Il n'a jamais eu l'imagination bien vive, ni ce feu d'esprit qui se remarque dans quelques-uns'; even as a child he played no games, was always 'doux, paisible et taciturne', and only learnt his letters at nine. But his father reflected that late fruit is rich fruit: 'On grave sur le marbre bien plus malaisément que sur le sable', and thus he felt confident that 'cette lenteur à comprendre, cette pesanteur d'imagination' was the sign of a ripening judgement, and indeed 'à force de battre le fer il en est venu glorieusement à avoir ses licences'. Is not this as good as Flaubert in its remorseless 'pondération'? The technique is so faultless that one finds oneself gazing apprehensively at the stupid boy, and reflecting that perhaps his looks belie him; 'there must be something' in what his father says. Joseph Prudhomme is pilloried here, along with the whole of modern 'fumisterie', the gullibility of the public and the adventitious methods of the advertiser.

A companion piece in its deliberate use of language as a means of mystification is the tactic of Tartuffe, when in his tightest corner. He uses words which are true, but which he would not for the world have accepted by others as true; he uses them because, and only because, they will be disbelieved. The trick is one that only a hypocrite can play, but it is important to see why it adds to the aesthetic enjoyment of the audience. When discovered by Damis in the act of making love to the wife of his host Tartuffe admits his guilt, in general terms so sweeping that they appear, not as fact, which they are, but as the fruit of humility. Thus by describing himself (to the joy of the audience) the rogue convinces the fool of the opposite. His dangerous tactic succeeds completely.

> Oui, mon frère, je suis un méchant, un coupable,
> Un malheureux pécheur, tout plein d'iniquité,
> Le plus grand scélérat qui ait jamais été,
> Chaque instant de ma vie est chargé de souillures . . . .

These statements are true, but they are the reverse of sincere. They overturn the universal assumptions of language; they are uttered not to persuade but to hoodwink. From this kind of man the truth is heard only when he can be certain that it will be taken for the opposite. With relentless dramatic skill Molière forces his rogue into a situation where he can and must show forth this paradox. And he pushes that situation to the extreme of tension. The hypocrite, sure of his case, dances on the tight-rope of his own astuteness. They must not be deceived, he says, by his appearance:

> Vous fiez-vous, mon frère, à mon extérieur?
> Et, pour tout ce qu'on voit, me croyez-vous meilleur?
> Non, non; vous vous laissez tromper à l'apparence,
> Et je ne suis rien moins, hélas, que ce qu'on pense.
> Tout le monde me prend pour un homme de bien
> Mais la vérité pure est que je ne vaux rien.

Can the mastery of irony go farther than to convict a criminal out of his own mouth and by his own tactic and desire? Is not this a new discovery in dramatic ambiguity? Molière here attains, it seems to me, that razor-edge of language which (*pace* Mr. Empson) it is not quite right to call ambiguity. For this statement cannot be taken in one of two or more ways; it has different meanings to different people, and in particular one meaning for the dupe and another for the audience. But the clarity is perfect; neither of the receiving parties is likely to understand it the wrong way: Tartuffe is sure of Orgon, and Molière is sure of his public.

The principle at work here is dramatic irony. This is used with remarkable consistency throughout Molière's comedy and no definition of his art can fail to include it as an ingredient. The dramatist makes his puppets say what, on reflection, they would not say. All of us are funny when we say what we do not mean, or when our speech, intending to convey definite meaning, conveys something more, or conveys precisely that which we would hide. This does not happen nearly so often in life as in Molière's plays. He puts his characters systematically, so to speak, into corners, situations where their speech, intending to be intelligent, is in fact instinctive, where they say more than they mean, or where they are not conscious of what they are saying. Does not comedy largely consist of this use of language against the intention of the user but obeying the intention of the dramatist? 'Je ne suis pas bon, je suis méchant quand je veux' is extracted from Argan, unwittingly, by a long process of contradiction. It is not what he would ever want to say. It is, however, a deeply true statement about him, and about all of us. Comic drama elicits the utterance of what in most of us is buried, suppressed, unutterable.

By such brilliant use of ironic language Molière was the liberator of his age. The practice of the society in which he moved covered the normal content of language with a social coating of convention. The phenomenon of politeness turns around this question of speech. In normal speech we should all maintain that we mean what we say, or at least that we say more or less what we mean. But social speech does almost the opposite. It conceals meaning and thus is a tyranny. Men have to say they are 'delighted' when they are not; they have to praise those whom they do not admire; they have to conceal their real feeling. Molière's drama, by exposing this tyranny, relieves us of its strain and shows us countless situations in which conventions of speech break down. He situates his characters so that the veneer of politeness peels off like a crust, so that their animosity may have free play. We have seen how Jourdain's teachers quarrel, and just so do Vadius and Trissotin, Célimène and Arsinoé. Even Alceste's courtesy is not proof against the fatuousness of Oronte, who asks point-blank whether his sonnet is a bad one, and thus forces Alceste into the series of excuses that begin with 'Je ne dis pas cela'. In other words, direct speech must be disavowed; one must say that one has not said it, or meant it. 'What do you mean?' becomes a key question. 'What should I mean', answers Angélique, direct and nettled, 'but what I say?' There is comedy, as Molière suggests in more than one place, in the very expression 'Je veux dire', in the necessity of saying what you say. Neither Alceste nor anyone else can tell when a society lady is sincere: 'De tout ce que j'ai dit, je me dédis ici.' Alceste is comic in that in such a society he admits no criterion but nature:

> Ce n'est que jeu de mots, qu'affectation pure,
> Et ce n'est point ainsi que parle la nature.

For a seventeenth-century gentleman this was an impossible position, and the fact that it is less so now means that the comedy loses something of its point.

Part of the comedy of Alceste lies in his use of the social language of his day. He adopts the clichés, but puts meaning into them. In this as in other respects he is individual, personal, refusing to conform to the social pattern. The gallants of his day spoke of 'mon faible', 'la chaîne qui m'attache' as almost meaningless clichés. For Alceste the same language will do, and it becomes, comically, meaningful. The intellectual, or doctrinaire, part of him actually does regard love as a weakness and fondness for the lady as a chain. In his mouth 'l'attachement' is no longer a cliché, but a description.

How is it that speech is thus so much more meaningful in Molière than in life? Do we not here approach one of the secrets of his art, something that is no merely superficial grace but the sign of a dynamic quality? Molière has left no treatise on language. We must assume the subtlety of his imaginative penetration into speech by his artistic use of it in character. One odd reference, however, suggests that he was perfectly aware of the delicacies and even of the philosophy of language. In a completely serious and personal piece of writing, the preface to *Tartuffe*, we find him making the statement that 'on doit discourir des choses et non pas des mots ... la plupart des contrariétés viennent de ne pas entendre et d'envelopper dans un même mot des choses opposées ... il ne faut qu'ôter le voile de l'équivoque.' This is not only a description of the accomplishment of his own dramatic irony; it is an admission that should be placed where I think it belongs, beside the arguments of Pascal in the fragment on *L'Esprit Géométrique*. Both men discerned the fatal flaw in reasoning that originates in the fact that the same thing may be understood in different ways. Language as disguise: Molière could not remain blind to this while he unmasked so many social disguises. Does not 'la dévotion' in his play mean different things to different people? What was a *libertin*? Cléante complains that 'c'est être libertin que d'avoir de bons yeux'. It is all a question of what you mean. What you intend to say and what you do say are often quite different. In speech as in act there may rise to the surface with or without our knowledge fragments of the subterranean world in every man. As another contemporary said: 'Il s'en faut que nous connaissions toutes nos volontés.'

V. SCENE

It is open to question whether any inquiry into principles of dramatic structure is in the case of writers such as Molière likely to yield results of any value. Imagining his life as actor-manager, rehearsing and adapting material at high speed, one cannot think of his own plays being written other than hurriedly. We are not surprised at his borrowing, not only themes but scenes, from other plays, including his own. The fact that should surprise us is the astonishing durability and vitality, through many generations of acting and reading, of what must have been so rapidly composed.

Yet those who do not think of works of art as composed by magic have to find some answer to the question as to how these comedies were put together. Most scholars seem either to have left this question on one side, or to have been satisfied to remark that for Molière plot was of secondary importance and that he preferred to concentrate upon character and realistic observation. But neither of these things is a principle of play-making. Drama is after all an imitation of human action; in a play something happens, something that, as Aristotle said, has beginning and end. Character, realism, these are not things that happen; they do not start or finish. They furnish material, which has somehow to be arranged. Nature does not, even for a Frenchman, make five neat acts. The artist does so, but only by a tortuous process of selection and omission and fusion. Admittedly we cannot follow this process; we have no instruments to plot imaginative creation and gestation. But we may at least remind ourselves of its existence.

Molière's early plays show quite clearly that he found difficulty in providing plays of the length and type that his audience wanted. He attempted the full-length comedy in verse, before his return to Paris, in the manner of the elegant comedy of his day. But his own first success was scored with a brief farce, his next with *Les Précieuses Ridicules* in one act, the next with a three-act play in verse. Only with *L'École des Femmes* did he achieve a five-act verse comedy in his own manner, and even then thanks to an intricate and improbable plot. The action of the play *L'Étourdi* was, as its sub-title indicates, a series of 'contretemps' woven into a *comédie à tiroirs*, the elastic type of play which could be extended according to the ingenuity of the author and the patience of the audience. That of *L'École des Femmes* depends on the accidents and incidents which enable a scheme to be defeated, and the denouement is brought about by a fantastic arrival of long-lost parents from overseas. It could not be said that by 1662 Molière had discovered how to construct a play otherwise than by a complicated plot.

Yet his training as a *farceur* had furnished him with certain elements of dramatic structure. From the earliest times comedy had been concerned with everyday life; the stuff of which it was made was by tradition the doings of ordinary people in ordinary surroundings. As Gilbert Murray writes, in the essay already quoted on Menander: 'Tragedy, to use the old Roman division, dealt with Res Sacra; the comedy of Aristophanes dealt with Res Publica; that of Menander was occupied with Res Privata, a region in which the emotions and changes of fortune may be smaller in extent, but are infinitely more various' (p. 26). *Res privata*: this gave to comedy both the setting and the characters. Molière's plays deal with the stock comic characters, in everyday situations: parents, children, the doctor, the schoolmaster, the soldier, the valet, relatives, in-laws, suitors. Like his contemporaries, he dealt with family problems, such as marriage, which would bring young and old into conflict, or infidelity, which would play off man and wife.

In some plays Molière is satisfied to reproduce comic situations of this sort. Both the *Précieuses* and *Dandin* turn on the wrong choice of marriage partners. The greater plays frequently portray a single family, which tyranny or stupidity has turned upside down. The sign of this is usually a love match resisted by the parents. Thus Philaminte wants a pedant, and Argan a doctor, for son-in-law. Such themes suggest that for Molière plot was indeed secondary, and that he preferred to reveal character and provoke laughter by exploiting stock situations rather than by inventing new material.

Yet all his plays have some plot. Things happen to the characters; the complications work out to some solution. But this plot is either episodic, as in *L'Avare*, in which Harpagon's loan to his son and the theft of his cash-box have little to do with each other. Or it is tenuous and unimportant, as in *Le Misanthrope*, in which Alceste is irritated by his lawsuit and exasperated by Célimène's letter given to him by Arsinoé. Or it amounts to little more than the stereotyped motif of marriage against the will of the parties, as in *Tartuffe* and *Les Femmes Savantes*. Obviously, therefore, the stuff that Molière put into his play is not in the actual plot.

What is meant by saying, as Tilley does, that in Molière's plays 'the conception of the living character preceded the search for a plot'? It suggests that the dramatist imagines or conceives a kind of person, and then fits to his conception such incidents as will make that person a true stage creation. It suggests in fact the opposite of a sequence of incidents leading logically to a conclusion. This would seem to apply to *L'Avare*, since the loan to the son, the supper-party, and the theft can be taken as mere instances strung together to convey in dramatic form a miser such as Molière had conceived him. But such a view raises more difficulties than it solves. Psychology is not drama. Few people can have read or watched Molière's plays without feeling the impression of dramatic power. Psychology in dramatic form is no valid explanation of works of art such as the greater comedies. To say that character conditions structure is in effect to reduce *Le Misanthrope* to a series of dramatic illustrations of a certain type of misanthropy. It is not so that the great dramas of the world have come to life.

If then we find neither in plot nor in character an organic principle of dramatic structure, where are we to look? Where indeed, but in the workshop of Molière himself? Did the tradition of the French farce offer him nothing but a setting? Did it not provide a rough-and-ready method of play-making? Here is a suggestion of what Molière may have seen and loved as a boy:

'Que ce soit sur les tréteaux, en plein air, ou, en dépit de ses grandes tragi-comédies, à l'Hôtel de Bourgogne, la faveur du public allait surtout, jusque pendant l'enfance de Molière, à la vieille farce française, peinture de la bêtise et de la ruse naïve, dans toutes les situations typiques de la vie, telle que l'avaient faite déjà les fabliaux du moyen âge; il s'agissait de tours de fripons, de maris trompés, le tout agrémenté d'ivrognes et de coups de bâton . . . un paysan épouse une femme au-dessus de sa condition . . . une paysanne, pour se venger des coups de son mari, l'enferme par surprise dans un sac et le fait vendre à la foire comme un cochon; une autre désigne son mari comme un médecin fameux mais qu'il faut contraindre par des coups de bâton à exercer son art.'

Here, recognizably, are Molière's themes. Has he worked them into plays by other methods than those by which they were already made amusing? Are not his own plays constructed on this rather gross basis of 'la peinture de la bêtise et de la ruse'? 'Le principal thème du comique de Molière est le jeu entre la sottise et la ruse', says the same scholar.[1] The dynamic principle of both the French farce and the *commedia dell' arte* is perhaps found here, in the hands of two classic comic figures, the fool and the rogue. Consider how

[1] Vedel, op. cit., p. 476.

many of Molière's plays elaborate the same 'donnée'. The various Sganarelles are, as the name perhaps implies, so many disguises of the fool: a valet, a coward, a husband maybe, but always fooled, deceived, outwitted. Are not Orgon, Jourdain, and Dandin fooled in similar fashion?

The counterpart, and often the complement, of the fool is the rogue. Mascarille is the obvious example: 'Vivat Mascarillus, fourbum imperator.' Or Sbrigani, described as 'Napolitain, homme d'intrigue', and Scapin 'valet de Léandre et fourbe'. On a grander scale but fulfilling the same function we find Arnolphe, Tartuffe, Don Juan, and the doctors.

This anatomy of trickery, this struggle between deceiver and deceived, is rudimentary as a principle of psychology but unfailing as a dramatic agent. When conducted with verve it can replace plot. In the *Précieuses Ridicules*, for example, the plot is largely an impersonation conducted by Mascarille. In *Tartuffe* the plot is the attempt of a sinister 'fourbe' to outwit a whole family. The plot of *Le Malade Imaginaire* is, as we shall see, little more than the various gullibilities of a hypochondriac. Argan and Alceste are superior types of Sganarelle. 'Sganarelle et Alceste, voilà tout Molière', said Sainte-Beuve.

This is not to deny that in such a creation as Alceste we see an almost incredible refinement and metamorphosis of the fool of the old comedy. Hardly less so is the rogue transformed, from a figure of fun, into such complex social types as Tartuffe and Don Juan. Moreover, the two comic types are not only astonishingly developed, they are fused. Argan is both tyrannical and gullible. Arnolphe and Tartuffe, deceivers both, are in the end both deceived. And even this progression is not away from farce but back to its genius. Audiences have always been incited to laugh at 'le trompeur trompé', at the schemer hoist with his own petard.

In the working out of the conflict between cunning and foolishness Molière arranges his characters into two or three groups. Some plays present opposing groups of characters, on the one side those who are right, on the other those who are wrong. *Tartuffe* is an example of this grouping. In *Le Misanthrope* there would seem to be three groups, Célimène and Oronte representing one extreme view, Alceste and Arsinoé another, Éliante and Philinte a middle position. In pointing this out M. Michaut suggests that this new structural feature is due to the fact that the dramatist was forced to declare his own view, and to guard himself by some expression of sound sense against the accusation of siding either with the deceivers or with the deceived. One or more characters, therefore, stand apart from the action, in the manner of the ancient chorus, and act as mouthpiece of the author. This raises an interesting point of structure. The character usually known to critics as 'le raisonneur' appears in many plays. Is he a subjective and politic intrusion, or an artistic necessity?

Is it certain, in the first place, that such characters do express the author's mind? Many scholars are persuaded that they do.

Jamais Molière n'a dissimulé son opinion personnelle; toujours, au contraire, il a chargé un de ses personnages, et quelquefois plusieurs, de le représenter et de l'exprimer très clairement . . . dans *L'École des Maris* Ariste, dans *L'École des Femmes* Chrysalde, dans *Le Tartuffe* Cléante, dans *l'Amour Médecin* Filerin, dans *Les Femmes Savantes* Henriette et Clitandre, dans *Le Malade Imaginaire* Béralde.[1]

The list is impressive. With the exception of Béralde all these characters express a normal and sensible view. But was it in any particular sense Molière's view? To say so is to brand him as a man of very ordinary and unexciting views. It is to open the door to Faguet's famous description of the leading French dramatist as a man of limited, bourgeois outlook, whose dominant idea was the golden mean. We know little of Molière's personal outlook but, as M. Mornet has recently suggested, the scanty evidence available points to the very opposite of a lover of the golden mean. His life

---

[1] Michaut, *Les Luttes de Molière*, p. 227.

was that of a man who threw caution to the winds, who was far more imaginative and daring than he was prudent. Of all the *raisonneurs* Béralde is the only one who does not express moderate views, and there is some evidence that Molière himself did not share them, but took the advice of a doctor.

So there may after all be no need to imagine Molière taking such care to keep a mouthpiece for himself. These characters have a better reason for their presence, an aesthetic reason. They ensure symmetry and roundness of comic presentation. Excess is the more distinguishable if its opposite is exhibited at the same time. Sense shows up nonsense, sobriety offsets bad temper. To insist that one should be 'sage avec sobriété' is a piece of rather flat moralizing unless and until it is put in contrast to a man doing the precise opposite. Cléante praises 'la dévotion humaine et traitable', surely not because Molière was anxious to show that he approved of that kind of piety, but because the artistic opposite of Tartuffe's exaggerated and false piety is precisely that. The colourless nature of such statements by the *raisonneurs* marks the degree of excess in the rogues and fools: if it indicates any one point of view it is that of the average spectator for whom the show is devised, rather than that of the author.

It is time to look more closely at the type of play which Molière constructed on the elemental basis of the struggle between fraud and foolishness. Since he died at the height of his powers his last play will form a good example; it is his ultimate case of dramatic structure. We may remind ourselves that no less a judge than André Gide has found it to be the most daring and remarkable of his plays. The plot of *Le Malade Imaginaire* might be summarized thus: Argan, the hypochondriac, decides to marry his daughter to a doctor and to leave his money to his second wife rather than to the children of his first. He is persuaded to feign death and thus discovers that his wife has no affection for him and his daughter has much. Persuaded further to defy his doctors and to listen to a new one (really his servant in disguise), he is finally cajoled into taking part in a burlesque ceremony whereby he is himself admitted to the medical profession. Considered as plot, this is more than slight; it is disjointed, episodic, and rather pointless.

Nor does the play make much better sense if considered as a comedy of character. Part only of the action portrays the hypochondria. It is sometimes assumed that the rest is farcical padding for cheap entertainment, liberally seasoned with satire against doctors.

The difficulty clears as soon as one ceases to look at either the plot or the title role as determining the structure of the play. If the main episodes be treated as equally important a rather different picture of the dramatic subject emerges. These episodes appear to be seven in number:

A. Argan, alone and in the presence of his doctors.
B. Diafoirus, father and son, making a good impression with a view to a contract of marriage between the son and Argan's daughter.
C. Béline, protesting affection and endeavouring to oust Angélique from the family fortune.
D. Toinette, impersonating a new and more wonderful doctor.
E. Béralde, arguing that one should trust nature rather than doctors.
F. Cléante, suitor to Angélique, and impersonating a music teacher.
G. Louison, fooling her father.

Whereas only two, or at most three, of these episodes illumine the theme of hypochondria, all of them are cases (except E) of what might be called double identity. Argan, by nature a healthy man, is persuaded to act as if he were ill. Diafoirus père devotes all his energies to proving that black is white. His son is a nitwit pretending to be clever. Béline protests an affection she is all too ready to disavow. Toinette adopts a disguise that deceives nobody but her master. The suitor gets into the house under false pretences. Louison feigns death. Argan's doctors parade a power they do not really possess. Only Angélique and Béralde are natural. All this deception centres upon Argan. We see him surrounded by people who, for their own profit or for his, are anxious to outwit him. And it is easily done; he is, one might say, the ideal subject. So that to think of the play as a satire on doctors is to consider only part of the evidence. The satire includes Béline, who has nothing to do with doctors; it includes doctors in a non-professional capacity: Diafoirus's attempts to marry off his impossible son are a clumsy way of satirizing the profession.

Surely the basic theme of a struggle between stupidity and fraud is nearer the mark; it covers every character, every scene. Looking closer, one can see that the 'fourbes' in the play have a common weapon. In a word that weapon is jargon. They rely for their power upon words; their words are not to be understood, but to be accepted because of those who say them. We who watch can see that the words are in every case belied by the facts, they are unsupported by evidence. But they are effective on one who wants to believe rather than to understand. Argan is taken in by the words of Béline, so much so that he pays no attention to the fact that she has brought a lawyer with her. He is taken in by the jargon of his doctors, so much so that he pays no attention to the evidence of his health: he walks without a stick, forgetting their instructions, and when Toinette reminds him that he cannot walk without a stick he admits that she is right. He is taken in by the childish trick of his younger daughter. He is taken in by the words of Diafoirus, even though standing before him is the living embodiment of crass stupidity.

The fact that the fool of the play, around whom swarm the rogues, is in the commanding position of head of the family means that he is the meeting-point of the schemers and their opponents. These latter are the necessary antithesis of the former. Their common feature is resistance to jargon, a refusal to be taken in by words, an ability to judge on evidence. They all distinguish, as Béralde explicitly does, between 'les discours' and 'les choses': 'Ce qu'il dit, que fait-il à la chose?' One of them, the servant, has the delightful and, in the setting of the play, the quite logical idea of carrying Argan's belief in professional opinion to the limit of absurdity, by dressing up as a doctor, by relating all his complaints and habits, including his good appetite and taste for wine, to an impossible cause, the lungs, and by recommending him, professionally, to have his arm off and his eye out.

Argan's appearances form no abstract study of hypochondria; they exhibit a person who believes whatever is said professionally, a slave to the magic of medicine. The mystery of science has an authority such that it will cover the most blatant nonsense. He believes that if the number of purges in a given month decreases his health will be correspondingly bad. He believes in the mystic power of medicine and of the medicine men: 'Je sens que la médecine se venge.' He believes that it matters if he walks *en long* rather than *en large*, that it matters how many grains of salt are put to his egg, that, in fact, everything matters if professionally sanctioned. Everything is mystery; as Béralde says, he sees things with strange eyes. His judgement is clouded and almost replaced by superstition: 'N'y a-t-il point quelque danger à contrefaire le mort?' Almost, but not quite; he has a remnant of common sense which can still discern between false and true. He can be persuaded to test Béline's affection and to let himself be enrolled as a doctor. But whether he can rid himself of the fear of 'science' we are not told.

All this is significant and not the haphazard work of a botcher of scenic effects. The effects are certainly gross; considered as a psychological study the play is at many points quite unconvincing. But it was not the author but academic critics who proclaimed it to be psychology and satire. All we can know of his intentions is given us in the form of the play as he wrote it. That form is so clear,

symmetrical, and indeed poetic that we should surely be able to gather
from it the main drift of the author's intention. We have seen that
all the situations are about the same thing; they all impinge on a
concept, which we may call by any of its aspects: jargon, words,
professionalism, trust in experts, superstition, or the mystery of
science, perhaps just 'Science'. Not only is there a single connecting
theme; the tone is maintained throughout, and it is not one of realism but of fantasy. The effects are quick and living, as in farce; the
point is obviously not in the motivation but in the suggestion of a
state of mind. That state of mind is always the same, the contrast
between words and evidence. Argan is one of Molière's 'imaginaires', he imagines the world other than it is for the majority of
us. In his case, as we watch those who exploit or befriend him, we
can see how vast and subtle a structure Molière has built upon the
ground-plan of farce. The fight between rogue and fool has here
broadened out to a suggestion, no more, of the gulf that separates
the mind from reality, the products of thought from the nature of
things. And the structure is episodic indeed, but with the connecting thread of a dominant concept. Realists would find every scene
faulty; the spectator content to watch the poetic play of fancy round
successive aspects of the subject is amazed at the way in which the
suggestive lightness of touch has enabled the artist to recover
liberty of treatment. The mixture of what is probable and what is
grotesque or macabre or sinister is more than any conscious mixture;
it is a new creation of the dramatic imagination.

The *Malade Imaginaire* shows Molière's art at its full maturity.
Its loose and poetic structure is proof that the play is not built as a
study in psychology. Nor is it built as a satire, although it contains
some obvious (and harmless) satire. The speed and fantasy with
which the whole subject is covered is a structural design which
deserves study. Molière has in this play illustrated an alternative to
the usual step-by-step method of building up a dramatic action.
This new principle of structure might be said to depend on suffusion

rather than on deduction. The loosely linked scenes all stand in direct relation to the master concept; they build up a vision not of a person nor of a plot but of a choice of attitudes. To borrow a phrase of Pascal: 'Cet ordre consiste principalement à la digression sur chaque point qui a rapport à la fin, pour la montrer toujours.'[1] Perhaps one of the unexplained secrets of our enjoyment of Molière is his art of relating each detail and episode to the complete picture.

It may be helpful to apply these considerations to an earlier and even more subtle play. The subject of the structure of *Le Misanthrope* can now, thanks to a recent and masterly edition, be approached afresh. M. Rudler discerns four elements which go to make up the plot: the theme of social hypocrisy, the practice of a society salon, the love theme, and the lawsuit. Each element may be said to be progressively revealed, but not on any register of a progression in time, from cause to effect: they appear as successive illuminations of facets, of aspects.

The problem of structure is that of the relationship of these reappearing elements. It is easy, by isolating this or that aspect (which involves treating the others as subordinate), to make it appear that one theme dominates the rest. It is harder to maintain intact the variety of Molière's fresco and yet to find the unity which the spectator feels but which he cannot explain. Why, for example, are we as fascinated by the third act, in which Alceste hardly appears at all, as by the first and the fifth, where he is present all the time? What is the imaginative centre from which all parts of the play derive their vitality?

At first sight one might agree that the character of Alceste forms the centrifugal point. Everything that happens seems to converge upon him: he is the keystone of the dramatic edifice. For the first two acts, moreover, the play unfolds as an exploration into the secrets and consequences of his attitude. There is no need to praise yet again the marvellous exposition, as full, as swift, and as

[1] *Pensées*, ed. Cluny, No. 257.

symbolical as the first act of *Tartuffe* which evoked the outspoken admiration of Goethe. By the end of the opening scene all the issues of the play have been raised: temper, social criticism, the lawsuit, the love affair. And the stage is set for the progressive testing out of Alceste's theories, in a first frivolous skirmish with Oronte, in a *tête-à-tête* with Célimène and finally, with full orchestra, so to speak, in a crowded salon. One may notice as a feature of dramatic structure that through these first two acts the situation is steadily unveiled; there is no action in the usual sense. A canvas is rolled back, in conversations so momentous that they seem to be events.

But what is revealed, the character, or the situation? The distinction is important in view of the fact that with the third act the revelation of the situation continues but that of the character is interrupted. Those critics for whom the second revelation is the real subject speak of the scenes with the Marquis and Arsinoé as 'rest-scenes'; the term implies an attitude to the subject and to the construction of the play. It is a rash thing to assume that the function of a delightful third act is no more than 'repose'. Must not any true definition of the subject include these scenes? They are rich in comic material. The famous tirade of Acaste is almost pure comedy; the ladies' quarrel is the most vigorous scene in the play. It is vital to determine whether structurally they advance the subject, or do little more than fill out what we know already.

Consider the first scene in Act III. No doubt the pact on which the Marquis agree is a factor of the plot. But is there not a familiar ring about the attitude of Acaste?

> Quelque rare que soit le mérite des belles
> Je pense, Dieu merci, qu'on vaut son prix comme elles.

Is this not akin to the insistence of Alceste himself, in his desire to be appreciated ('Je veux qu'on me distingue'), and to his hot assertion that 'Je ne l'aimerais pas si je ne croyais l'être'? We are here, no less than in Act I, probing the depths from which the misanthropic mood may spring. Acaste shows as clearly as Alceste that personal vanity enters into any individual's estimate of any situation.

If this first scene enriches the theme how much more do the later scenes, especially the fifth? This cannot be read as mere relief, or as merely incidental to Arsinoé's pursuit of Alceste, which is essential to the plot. The situation is typical in its portrayal of an antagonism barely contained by the (obligatory and perfunctory) formulae of politeness. What the ladies think is almost as plain as if it had been explicit in words. We have here, in masterly form, a reproduction of scenes like that in the *Bourgeois Gentilhomme* where the teachers start politely and end in blows, and that in the *Femmes Savantes* where the poets observe the conventions until their feelings get the better of them and they quarrel like fishwives. But the sense and point of this particular quarrel is that it occurs in a play about plain speech. Arsinoé is an Alceste *retourné*; she too believes in saying what she means, and she does so, spitefully. Her *démarche* is the most mordant possible comment on the policy of one who desired 'qu'en toute rencontre Le fond de notre cœur dans nos discours se montre'. As such it brings powerful support to the attitude of a Philinte. Here is sincerity, and it is more disagreeable than Alceste ever realized it might be. The very words of the opening scene are taken up and echoed.

> Quoi, vous iriez dire à la vieille Émilie
> Qu'à son âge il sied mal de faire la jolie
> Et que le blanc qu'elle a scandalise chacun?

In Philinte's mind this was an hypothesis; in the mouth of Célimène it is fact, and is passed back to the person who does it:

> Mais elle met du blanc et veut paraître belle.

Conversation of this sort is dangerous; the victim finds it wounding, bitter, strangely irritating (963–4). It leads to that most sensitive of all subjects for society women, a comparison of ages. Not only so, but under pressure of hatred and spite, Célimène expresses Alceste's own position, that truth should be told in society:

> Au contraire, Madame, et si l'on était sage,
> Ces avis mutuels seraient mis en usage;
> On détruirait par là, traitant de bonne foi,
> Ce grand aveuglement où chacun est pour soi.

Such words are a brilliant illumination of the central issue of the play. This 'renversement du pour au contre' shows us the coquette herself in the heat of the moment putting into practice Alceste's high-flown demand. But it is far more than Alceste's character that is here illumined; it is an issue, the issue of how principles fare in a hard world. To make this great play a study of character is to limit the range of its drama. The whole question of the nature of sincerity, involving as it does vanity, fashion, spite, convention—it is this complex of questions that conditions the order and structure of the play. The scheme of construction is once again, as in the *Malade*, suffusion, poetic presentation of an abstract issue in concrete pictures. One cannot expect such elusive and ethereal matter to be presented in the time-sequence of a plot. It has been well said that this play 'n'avance pas sur la corde raide d'une logique uni-linéaire; le fil en est quelquefois invisible . . . elle se calque sur la vie, dont elle reproduit l'allure et jusqu'au secret'.[1]

Are we not now in a position to give to the expression 'comédie de caractère' a fuller meaning? Molière's creations of this kind seem to revolve around a single character, which is not presented with any Shakespearian fullness but with certain features powerfully illuminated. These are in themselves abstract qualities such as hypocrisy, timidity, bad temper, pedantry, which, though abstract, come to life in the conflict of certain social situations. Such a play will show the meeting of the idealist and the fop, the coquette and the cross-grained spinster; it will not present any full character study of an idealist. The successive scenes do not so much narrate events

[1] Ed. Rudler, p. xxiii.

as expose an attitude and a relationship. The basic relationship is that between the mask and the face.

These are the factors which condition the structure of the comedies: as a basis the antinomy of fools and rogues, as setting the conditions of bourgeois life, usually within a family, as incident, a sequence of scenes loosely linked into a kaleidoscope or film of human attitudes. We are shown, not the time-progression of a Tartuffe through triumph to failure, but rationally selected aspects of his humanity, which make up, not the complete hypocrite but a symmetrical vision of the comic disproportion that we call hypocrisy. The form is outwardly episodic; its links are internal, fibrous, poetic; it is what the Germans would call 'inner form'.

It is this inner cohesion, in fantasy rather than in realism, that explains the denouements for which Molière has been so criticized. Those accustomed to plays that proceed to a logical and inevitable end are scandalized by endings which are the reverse of inevitable, by unexpected police intervention, or arrival of long-lost parents, or by recognitions as far-fetched as any in ancient comedy. It is significant, however, that actors find these endings appropriate to the plays they terminate. Louis Jouvet has written: 'Il y a une certaine sottise et une certaine impertinence à parler de la pauvreté des dénouements de Molière; ils sont de la plus parfaite et de la plus fine convention théâtrale.' Perhaps here academic critics have something to learn from Molière's own profession. If such endings act well, should they not be regarded as the work of fancy rather than of logic? Is it not fantasy that produces the superb ending of the *Fourberies*, where Scapin, whose pretence of death has been only partly successful, insists on being carried to supper: 'Et moi, qu'on me porte au bout de la table, en attendant que je meure.' Fantasy is indeed highly appropriate to end a spectacle in which the distinction between the probable and the improbable is designedly vague, and in which any realistic happy ending would mean an alteration or violation of character. It has been truly said that in Molière's drama there are no eleventh-hour conversions; his fools remain fools, his rogues are unrepentant. It is no coincidence that so many plays finish in a last fanciful twist of imagination such as ballet, or mock ceremonies or fantastic make-believe. The muses of comedy, ballet, and music invade the stage and force Sganarelle, who has just discovered that he has really signed away his daughter, to dance with them as they sing:

> Sans nous tous les hommes
> Deviendront malsains,
> Et c'est nous qui sommes
> Leurs grands médecins.

VI. SCOURGE

'Never did man wield so shrieking a scourge upon vice.' Meredith's phrase sounds rhetorical, but he has found many to agree with him, who read some at least of the greater plays of Molière as if they were primarily satires, and only incidentally comic. Certain aspects of French life are indeed hit hard in the plays. The satire is at times contemporary to the point of being personal, at others directed against certain types of character: pedants, doctors, misers, hypocrites, sycophants. Some of these had been fair game in comedy for centuries. Of other types, lashed by his contemporaries, Molière has nothing to say. He did not satirize the law, nor financial dealers, nor (save gently in Jourdain) social climbers.

The plainest satire in Molière would seem to be that of the contemporary doctors, exposed for their ignorance, their jargon, and their dishonesty. In *L'Amour Médecin*, where four doctors compare notes about professional visits, where they quarrel and are rebuked by their senior for letting down the profession in the eyes of the public, there would seem to be clear reference to actual Paris practitioners. For the famous Diafoirus couple on the other hand no models are known. The satiric import is difficult to measure because, as with Molière's other rogues, they are never satirized apart from their victims. Which is held up to greater ridicule, the rogue or the dupe? The question suggests interesting conclusions about the structure of comedy. The satire on Argan is surely as keen as that on Purgon. The pedants who write bad verses are treated no more harshly than the girls gullible enough to praise them, Alceste is no more eccentric than Célimène or Arsinoé, Don Juan than Sganarelle.

This doubling of the satire has made some think that Molière is out to ridicule excess in any direction. The reasonable person found in most plays, whose job seems to be to supply counsels of good sense and moderation, has thus been taken to be the mouthpiece of the author. If this is so we have at least a standpoint from which the satire starts, so to speak. This tempts one to look at the *raisonneurs* for what the author approved, and at the fools and rogues for what he disapproved, and compose as Faguet did a list of his ideas. The result, as the previous chapter attempted to show, is proof of the folly of the proceeding.

So the question of what Molière thought is not so easy to answer as was imagined fifty years ago. But how else may we determine the import and even the nature of the satire? Granted that certain types are attacked, from what standpoint is the attack delivered, and what does it mean? Can we agree with John Palmer that 'the individual is derided as soon as his excess of character threatens to injure the social group'?[1] Is it not more likely that the standpoint of any play is that of the playgoer rather than that of the author? A comedian is not out to air his views but to please the public. He exhibits as funny what the audience will be expected to find funny. Of all dramatists the comic writer must be most anonymous and impenetrable behind his creation. As suggested elsewhere in these pages, to find what Molière thought we must go behind any set of views expressed to such a temperament as might create the sort of oppositions that he so often did create. Molière's view, as M. Benjamin once suggested, may be given by Agnès rather than by Arnolphe or Chrysalde. We cannot tell.

[1] *Comedy*, p. 14.

With this caveat in mind we may consider those plays in which there seems to be real satiric force. One of the most interesting and problematical, thanks to recent scholarship, is *Les Précieuses Ridicules*. As explained in the first chapter, this play can no longer be read as a satire on contemporary affectation of speech, still less as having been successful in curbing such affectation. There is no evidence that in 1659 any ladies in Paris or out of it talked as Cathos and Madelon did, just as there is no evidence that the real preciosity, which Molière's play hardly touched, was at all affected by its success. But as M. Adam has shown, *Les Précieuses Ridicules* was very probably, in its original form, a satire of a quite outspoken kind. Molière seems to have been engaged by the circle of the Grande Mademoiselle to lampoon that of Mlle de Scudéry, which enjoyed the patronage of Fouquet. Certain phrases are strangely similar to those used by Sapho in the *Grand Cyrus*. In the novel she expresses this view: 'Si je soupçonnais dans mon cœur un simple désir d'épouser quelqu'un je rougissais comme d'un crime.' This sounds very much like Madelon's horror of marriage. Like Mascarille, Sapho learnt all that she needed to know 'sans que l'on ait presque jamais ouï dire que Sapho ait rien appris'. More striking than these coincidences, however, was the satiric coupling of absurd speech and 'precious' manners, the suggestion that certain ladies of fashion lived in a quite unreal world of romance and premarital adventures. Their chief sin was to despise all things physical and 'earthy'. In the first version they refer by periphrasis to a commode; they declare the very notion of marriage to be absolutely shocking. One can imagine the *gauloiserie* that actors of farce would put into such a play, the zest with which Mascarille (Molière) would offer to undress in order to show them his wound. The actual undressing of the valets by the masters was in all probability a rough business and the vulgarity of the father may well have been enforced by wink and gesture.

It may seem far from the reasonable Molière of nineteenth-century text-books to the *farceur* who put on satire so direct and personal that it had to be toned down after the first few performances. But later evidence suggests that we must not lose sight of the rough-and-tumble atmosphere of his stage, nor of the habit of working off old scores by all too recognizable caricature. *Les Femmes Savantes* is a refined play, but it contains two caricatures that were immediately identified as of Cotin and Ménage. Vadius, representing Ménage, is pompous and undignified, but Trissotin is repulsive. The sonnet and epigram of Cotin which Trissotin claims to have written are said to have been supplied by Boileau, an old enemy. Perhaps such direct mockery seems more libellous now than it did then, but clearly Molière was not, as used to be thought, above the battle; he was in the arena with the rest. These two pedants, the précieuses, and the doctors in *L'Amour Médecin*, all cases of personal attack, suggest that other characters may be equally spiteful cartoons of contemporaries. But then, if this were the case, the fact would probably have been commented on by the gazetteers or by Molière's critics.

Was Tartuffe modelled from life? Before we discuss the question let us be clear that the play was banned as a satire. The fact that Molière kept up the fight for five years is clear evidence that he refused to soften or abandon the satire. In his final preface of 1669 he admitted as much. This document carries the attack still farther:

'Les hypocrites n'ont point entendu raillerie; ils se sont effarouchés d'abord et ont trouvé étrange que j'eusse la hardiesse de jouer leurs grimaces et de vouloir décrier un métier dont tant d'honnêtes gens se mêlent. C'est un crime qu'ils ne sauraient me pardonner. . . . Suivant leur louable coutume, ils ont couvert leurs intérêts de la cause de Dieu, et le *Tartuffe* dans leur bouche est une pièce qui offense la piété.'

All this goes very near the bone and could only be said when the issue had been decided, and by the man who had won and who no longer needed or cared to be diplomatic. There is no doubt that the play was offensive to religion, and was meant to be so. Its two leading characters are both outwardly pious, but one is a hypocrite and the other a bigot. The hypocrite is a scoundrel and a crook into the bargain.

We know what conclusions scholars have drawn from these facts. For one writer they prove that Molière was a free-thinker, notorious and proselytizing (*agressif*). For another they mark 'l'apogée du paganisme sous Louis XIV'. Such judgements assume precisely what is in debate, that in satirizing religion Molière declared his own disbelief in religion. But this is only one possible conclusion. There would seem to be two others. The play may be less impious and more satiric, an attack on religious people rather than on religion. Or, finally, the author may have thought that religious hypocrisy was a fit subject of comedy. On this alternative the religion would be incidental to the comedy; on the previous two, the comedy is incidental to the satire.

As to the first assumption, there is no evidence that Molière was a free-thinker. The views expressed in *Tartuffe* and *Don Juan* cannot be counted as evidence until the very problem we are confronted with has been settled. Until we can tell to what degree they reproduce Molière's own views they cannot be used as evidence. About Molière's religious views two things may be said with some certainty. He was not a practising Christian, whatever he may privately have thought, for the exercise of his profession made him excommunicate. Secondly, his profession as usually exercised would preclude him from airing his own opinions. Michaut has put this point cogently: 'Je voudrais savoir comment ce comique pouvait dans ses comédies témoigner de ses sentiments religieux. Et je voudrais bien qu'on me citât les auteurs de comédies classiques contemporains, antérieurs et postérieurs, qui l'ont fait.'[1]

As to the second alternative, it is quite possible that Molière intended to decry certain religious people, but it seems impossible to find out who they were. After M. Michaut's masterly review and rejection of the various candidates little remains to be said. The

[1] *Les Luttes de Molière*, p. 108 n.

Jesuits, whom the borrowing from *Les Provinciales* tempts us to think of first, the Jansenists with their outward austerity, the Compagnie du Saint Sacrement with their system of lay direction, any or all of these may have contributed features to Tartuffe, but none so many or so marked that one may say that they and not the others served as prototype. The author is a suspect witness, but he said in the most explicit terms that he had taken every care to avoid confusion with any model of true piety, and it would seem that he has succeeded. Indeed, the nearest one can get to a possible model would seem to be the hypocrite of whom Tallemant has left a sketch, Charpy, Sieur de Sainte Croix, who lived in Molière's own street, who was a crook and whose practices were very like those of Tartuffe:

Charpy se met si bien dans l'esprit du mari et s'impatronise tellement de lui et de sa femme qu'il en a chassé tout le monde, et elle ne va en aucun lieu qu'il n'y soit, ou bien le mari. Mme Hansse qui a enfin ouvert les yeux en a averti son gendre; il a répondu que c'étaient des railleries et prend Charpy pour le meilleur ami qu'il ait au monde.[1]

Since nothing positive can be determined as to Molière's own religious views, and since his satire cannot be attached to any specific religious group, the third alternative demands the more serious consideration: that Molière chose and developed the subject as a comedy rather than as a satire. One cannot resist the impression that *Tartuffe* has been read as a satire because it was thought to overstep the bounds of comedy. That reason can no longer be valid for any who accept the argument of an earlier chapter, whereby *Tartuffe* is not an exception but a supreme achievement of comedy as Molière has created it. If the author himself had this conviction the fact would go farther to explain his persistence in the fight for its public performance than any fancied religious views or animosities. The most certain fact known about Molière tells us nothing about his ideas; it is his mastery of the art and practice of comedy. There is no need

[1] *Historiettes*, vii. 148, cit. Michaut, *Luttes*, p. 66.

to prove this; it is everywhere admitted. It should be the decisive factor in any argument about disputed passages in his work.

On this reading, therefore, the models of *Tartuffe* are to be sought, not in parties or personalities of the French Church, but in humbler anonymous cases like that of Charpy. There have always been people who have used the externals of religion as a cloak, and the French have been keen to expose them. Molière's master Montaigne said that 'il n'y a aucune qualité si aisée à contrefaire que la dévotion', and among the artists Mathurin Régnier, Voltaire, Stendhal, Balzac, and Anatole France have all left evidence that they agreed with him. Molière's masterly picture should be interpreted as theirs have been. His models were possibly just as he described them:

> Ces gens qui par une âme à l'intérêt soumise
> Font de dévotion métier et marchandise,
> Et veulent acheter crédit et dignités
> A prix de faux clins d'yeux et d'élans affectés. (368)

But this is not to say that the play contains no satire. Granted that it portrayed a religious criminal, the attitudes and arguments of such a figure could not but delight the enemies of religion and correspondingly depress its defenders. The strength of the case against Molière lies in the fact that whatever he may have meant, the figure of his hypocrite, once it had become public property by being put, in flesh and blood as it were, on the stage, was no longer restricted by any intentions or safeguards. It was there for all to see, and to interpret as they liked. Herein lies its satiric force. Any who read or watched it might the more easily imagine any kind of piety as assumed, the more easily suspect externals as being outward show unaccompanied by conviction or humility. Molière could not get round the fact that certain attitudes are common both to piety and hypocrisy, and these attitudes would be met with in all kinds of religious profession, pastors and priests, monks and nuns, curés and archbishops. They are forcibly suggested in the play. It was not

only hypocrites who might protest that personally they would for-
give those who had done them wrong 'mais l'intérêt du Ciel n'y
saurait consentir' (1207). In the play the crook accepts property
because he fears

> Que tout ce bien ne tombe en de méchantes mains. (1244)

Did the Church of the day, with its dignities, pluralities, and fiefs,
seem to do anything else? Were not all 'directeurs de conscience'
under suspicion of acting covertly according to Tartuffe's explicit
methods?

> De ces secrets, Madame, on saura vous instruire;
> Vous n'avez seulement qu'à vous laisser conduire. (1493)

Finally, is not the sketch of Orgon a most direct satire on the
element of the unscrupulous associated with religious direction?
When asked if on religious grounds he is prepared to break his word
he hedges, leaving the questioner in no doubt. He uses the odious
argument that his daughter should mortify the flesh by accepting
her father's choice.

The satire is clear, and abundant, and we cannot assume that its
creator was blind to its presence. Yet we know that he risked his
professional standing and the future of his company by insisting
that his play be performed. Must we not say that his obstinacy, and
the sharpness of his satire, have a single cause? Surely only one
thing is adequate to explain this concurrence, and that is something
that for want of better words we may call the aesthetic necessity of a
true picture. 'Scélérat étonnant de vérité', such is Michaut's sum-
ming-up of Molière's hypocrite, and the phrase cannot be bettered.
But when we survey Molière's work as a whole we find this principle constantly active within it. One of its plainest characteristics
is the dislike of pretence, the sense of truth, in things as in people.
Here is the real source of all his satire, in the opposition of fact and
fancy, truth and falsehood. Flattery, compliments, tyranny, fraud,
all these appear in his drama as ripe for exposure against the truth.

And this is a feature of the work of his literary friends and contemporaries. The society in which they lived was built on appearance and riddled with deceit. 'On peut dire que le monde n'est composé que de mines', wrote one of them. They all exposed or commented on this pretence, as artists, that is, aiming not so much at improvement and reform as at truth of depiction. Molière is one of them, separated only by the finesse of his depiction. Truth to nature was his avowed principle: 'Lorsque vous peignez les hommes, il faut peindre d'après nature.' He fulfilled his own precept so vividly that a clever contemporary said that no plays seemed less like plays than his: 'Jusque là il y avait eu de l'esprit et de la plaisanterie dans nos comédies, mais il y ajoute une grande naïveté avec des images si vives des mœurs de ce siècle et des caractères si bien marqués que les représentations semblaient moins être des comédies que la vérité même.'[1]

It is clear that the same principles of criticism apply to *Don Juan* as to *Tartuffe*. Both plays were thought to be full of impiety. Both contain satire. Both raise the question of Molière's own ideas. In both is the satire apparently double in direction. As a bigot and a crook are exposed in the one, so a *libertin* and a fool are satirized in the other. The roles of both crook and *libertin*, if faithfully portrayed, contained dangerous material which it was thought immoral to publish.

The incentive to write a play on Don Juan is fairly clear. The theme was a contemporary success on the stage. It involved machines and the supernatural, which were no less popular. It was an obvious box-office choice, but none the less unfortunate. It evoked a howl of rage from the orthodox, had to be taken off, and could only be played in a bowdlerized version. We know of its content only by oblique references in a hostile pamphlet and a pirated Dutch edition twenty years after the event. The play divides the critics as no other does, except *Tartuffe*. It was for long

[1] Perrault, *Parallèles*, cit. Vedel, op. cit., p. 488.

dismissed as a hotchpotch and as a subjective outpouring of Molière's bitterness and disillusionment. There is now general agreement with Lemaître's view that it is at once one of the most suggestive of Molière's plays and 'obscure en diable'.

The obscurity is again connected with the question of the import of the satire. The play offers a full-length portrait of a *libertin*, vivid, and faithful to the fact. Don Juan is a dilettante, confident in his own powers. He admits neither revelation nor repentance. He rebuts the remonstrances of his valet, and delights to flout convention and morality. He respects no law or restraint upon his actions. His code is 'civilité', politeness without sincerity. The only external standard he respects is his reputation as a gentleman. 'Intrépidité, indépendance, voilà pour lui les qualités idéales du gentilhomme. Il ne reconnaît ni ne tolère aucune contrainte extérieure ou intérieure, ne craint ni Dieu ni diable, se refuse même à croire à l'un comme à l'autre: croire, c'est reconnaître, c'est accepter un lien.'[1]

This man comes to a bad end. But the fact did not soften the critics. It was, they said, 'obligatoire', a feature of the legend, under cover of which the dramatist might the more freely voice his own ideas.

Has Molière in fact done this? We know that he had no love for the Church, that he translated Lucretius, that *libertins* were among his friends. 'Chaque fois que l'on peut identifier et éclairer un cercle où Molière a pénétré, on y retrouve toujours les traces de La Mothe de Vayer et des disciples de Naudé et de Gassendi . . . on connaît trop bien ses attaches philosophiques.'[2] If this was so, the extraordinarily vigorous portrait of Don Juan may be due as much to sympathy as to satire. On the other hand, it is difficult to imagine Molière being foolhardy enough to use the stage as a vehicle for his own ideas in a realm where they were so dangerous and so likely to evoke hostility. The biographical evidence is not sufficient to settle the point. What

[1] Vedel, op. cit., p. 363.
[2] Mongrédien, *La Vie littéraire au xviie siècle*, pp. 332–3.

may we learn from the play? In the case of *Tartuffe* we have suggested that there is no need to read it as a tract, since it was more likely to be a work of dramatic imagination. Its main features and structure fit into a framework primarily aesthetic and not subjective or satiric. Can this be said also of *Don Juan*? Does it stand on its own feet as a play, conceived in the manner in which the other great comedies of its author would seem to have been conceived? Our original question recurs in a new form: is this work of art better and more fairly interpreted as a comedy or as a satire?

A first step towards an answer is to notice that the portrait of Don Juan is not the only detailed one in the play. No less striking, and surely no less true, is that of his servant, a monument of timorous and very human superstition. Sganarelle may have all the right ideas about morality but he holds them in an unintelligent, inconsequent, and gullible way. He believes in doctors as he believes in God and the devil, and on the same footing as the Deity he puts goblins like 'le moine bourru'. Here is satire, the truth of which was not denied. The complaint was that in Sganarelle Molière confides the cause of God to a dolt. But we do not believe, as Molière's critics believed, that a comedian has anything to do with putting the cause of God, and that even when one character attacks the Deity another should produce the best arguments to refute him. It was certainly risky to make the *libertin* intelligent and the pious man a fool. If the play were a tract, this would be a serious point; if it is a comedy, it is hardly relevant.

We have then two portraits, contrasted at almost every point throughout the play. Is it sufficient to say, as M. Michaut suggests, that both are true pictures and that Molière may have wished to do no more than 'faire vrai'? In the light of his principles of comic structure the contrast itself is likely to be of vital importance. This play is built round the relationship of master and man. It frequently suggests the prototype, which may well have been known to Molière, of Don Quixote. The *hauteur* of the master is paralleled by the grovelling of the man, the free thought of the one by the bondage to cliché and magic of the other, the freedom of the lord by the bondage of the servant. Is it an accident that both lie, the master because he thinks he need not observe the bourgeois habit of telling the truth, the servant because he is economically prevented from telling the truth? He would lose his job if he did. And very comically he does say what he thinks when he imagines that his master is out of hearing. As the master believes nothing, the man believes almost anything. The master scorns the marriage law; the man obeys it. The master never fears the consequences; the man always does. The master thinks nothing of 'what people say'; the man believes what 'they always say', that *libertins* come to no good end. The master turns out to be wrong and the man to be right.

Surely this contrast is motivated with such care and balance that it should not be ignored. What it comes to is nothing less than a dialogue on humanity. The master is inhuman in his scorn of others. The man is all too human. As we listen to him saying 'Pour moi, Monsieur, je n'ai point étudié comme vous, Dieu merci, et personne ne saurait se vanter de m'avoir rien appris, mais avec mon petit sens, mon petit jugement, je vois les choses mieux que tous les livres', as we imagine this said by Molière on his own stage, are we not forcibly reminded of the opposition in *L'École des Femmes*? Is not the comic dramatist weighting the scales in order to create the comedy of the inhuman, not merely opposed to the human but in need of the human? There are glimpses of humanity in this Don Juan, in his courage, in his silence before the statue, in his pity, in his choice of a valet. But his code is an inhuman one of self-sufficiency, and therein he shows himself more small-minded than the veriest fool. 'Rien n'accuse davantage une extrême faiblesse d'esprit que de ... faire le brave contre Dieu.'[1] There is nothing in the play to show that

[1] *Pensées*, ed. minor, p. 422. Cf. La Bruyère: 'L'esprit fort, c'est l'esprit faible.'

Molière does not agree with Pascal here, and that he was not constructing his picture on similar lines.

The satire is not diminished by being subordinated to this principle of comic structure. It is biting and relevant in the case of both master and man. But it is set in a frame that is more than satiric, a frame of irony, that sees the *libertin* not as impious in his daring, but as misguided in his self-confidence, that sees him cut off from his fellows. Like Harpagon, Don Juan is alone in his world, despising the company of both God and man. As such he is foolish where he thinks he is superior. 'C'est une grande folie de vouloir être sage tout seul.' As so often, La Rochefoucauld supplies the marginal comment and Molière the dramatic and poetic creation.

VII. SMILE

THE previous chapters on Molière's use of gesture, mask, word, and scene may serve as convergent considerations enabling us now to attack a central question hitherto avoided, concerning the nature of the comedy which Molière created. It is the function of criticism to explain the general reference of particular works of art. In the case of comedy this has resulted in the (surely comic) situation of generalizing a theory of the comic and applying it with drastic results to the masters of comedy. 'On voit toute la vanité de la méthode qui consiste à déterminer l'idée de la comédie pour montrer que Molière est, ou n'est pas, comique.'[1] Another procedure hardly more legitimate is to see in Molière or Shakespeare the norm of comedy by which other writers may be judged. The present inquiry is concerned to elucidate what in the case of a single artist are the particular forms of that general attitude which corresponds to the word 'comic'. It rests upon the assumption that comedy for Molière was an end and not a means. This is not the view usually held outside France. English and German writers have admitted his keen sense of the ridiculous, but see it always harnessed to a doctrine or to an attack on social abuses. But are we not on firmer ground in claiming as the secret of Molière's popularity an artistic

[1] Stapfer, *Molière et Shakespeare*, 1880, p. 114.

vision that must not be confused either with ideas or with satire, and that in his work we may look for what M. Arnavon has called 'du comique, du comique partout, parfaitement accessible et que rien n'autorise à transposer'?[1]

It may well be that although his work has a comic appeal now as it had nearly three hundred years ago the same things are not found comic. What brought a laugh in 1670 may not bring one now. What was not then intended to be funny may have become so, through change of taste or by the growing weight of acting tradition. Even the word 'comédie' had in the seventeenth century two meanings, to one of which nothing that we call comic was attached. It was the general word for a play of any kind. Mme de Sévigné called *Bajazet* without disrespect 'une comédie'. This sense survives in the expressions 'aller à la comédie' and 'La Comédie Française'. A second sense referred to the type of play that was the counterpart of tragedy, a play with ordinary characters, homely language, and a theme that might be anything that was not serious.

Contemporary references make it clear that Molière put new content into this second sense of the word. Crowds filled his theatre, not to see merely the fanciful, the exaggerated, the absurd, or the romantic, but to laugh. He was called 'le premier farceur de France' and 'le dieu des ris'. Discerning observers testified to the presence of other elements in his plays, but all were agreed that they made people laugh.

But what did a seventeenth-century audience laugh at? It is rather surprising that the point has not been investigated. We know from other comedies that they laughed at the eternal comic situations: beatings, disguises, mistaken identity, wit, buffoonery, indecency. The scenes and quips of Tabarin, for example, show all these features. The most obvious difference between them and the comedies of Corneille and Molière is that the latter achieved their object without indecency. Corneille abandoned the tone and

---

[1] *Molière notre contemporain*, p. 219.

atmosphere of farce altogether; Molière kept the roughness and boisterous fun; both kept to a decency of expression that is surprising even if one remembers that their audiences were relatively refined. For these same people delighted in literature that was not refined, that displayed a crudity of language and gesture which are notably absent from Molière's plays. It is true that his enemies made much of the famous 'le' in *L'École des Femmes*; there is a (small) amount of 'lavatory' humour in two plays, and some indecent gesture in *Le Médecin malgré lui*, but that is all—in the text. Even allowing for actors' gestures and insinuations the purification of dramatic diction by Molière is an unusual feature of his work.

But seventeenth-century laughter could be both crude and heartless. 'There are many laughters', writes J. C. Gregory, and he quotes Hobbes and Fuller as finding mirth in the fact of physical infirmity: 'When the Philistine lords made sport of blind Samson, they were mocking an enemy.'[1] We know from Molière's own text that Harpagon's delirious search for a thief provoked laughter. According to Sarcey some revengeful lines in *Tartuffe* did so still in 1890. He claims that the loudest laughter greeted Orgon's taunt after the exposure: 'Ah, ah, l'homme de bien, vous m'en voulez donner.' Arnolphe and Dandin were probably figures of fun merely because they were cuckolds:

> S'il faut que sur vous on ait la moindre prise
> Gare qu'aux carrefours on ne vous tympanise.

If Alceste appears to us a subtle and poetic character let us not forget that Molière's public found him an oddity for having the ridiculous notion that in society one can say what one means:

> Je vous dirai tout franc que cette maladie
> Partout où vous allez donne la comédie.

Mme Jourdain makes it clear that it was not for the naïve phrases at which we smile that her husband was thought funny, but for

---

[1] *The Nature of Laughter*, 1924, p. 9.

aping the gentry. He very naturally retorts that only fools will laugh at him for a fool:

MADAME: Vous moquez-vous du monde, de vous être fait enharnacher de la sorte? et avez-vous envie qu'on se raille partout de vous?

MONSIEUR: Il n'y a que des sots et des sottes, ma femme, qui se railleront de moi.

MADAME: Vraiment, on n'a pas attendu jusqu'à cette heure, et il y a longtemps que vos façons de faire donnent à rire à tout le monde.

MONSIEUR: Qui est donc tout ce monde-là, s'il vous plaît?

MADAME: Tout ce monde-là est un monde qui a raison, et qui est plus sage que vous.

It is not by accident that the butts in the comedy are told that they will be laughed at; the taunt has its full effect only if they are laughed at, as we may be sure they were.[1] Such passages show the comic dramatist at work, selecting the situations that would appeal, not to his own sense of humour so much as to that of his audience.

But we must proceed to examine those other passages which have suggested to the critics that Molière was not writing in the first place to evoke laughter. In his first published preface, in 1660, for example, he defended his play *Les Précieuses Ridicules* as an honest satire, in the true comic tradition:

'Ces vicieuses imitations de ce qu'il y a de plus parfait ont été de tout temps la matière de la comédie . . . les véritables savants et les vrais braves ne se sont point encore avisés de s'offenser du Docteur de la comédie et du Capitan; non plus que les juges, les princes et les rois, de voir Trivelin ou quelque autre sur le théâtre faire ridiculement le juge, le prince ou le roi.'

There is nothing here as to any purpose of comedy. Molière claims to be returning to its stock amusements. The famous discussion on the rules of art in the *Critique de l'École des Femmes* culminates in the statement that the rules should be regarded as no more than

---

[1] Cf. *supra*, p. 36, for the information, given by the miser himself, that Harpagon was laughed at.

'quelques observations aisées que le bon sens a faites sur ce qui peut ôter le plaisir que l'on prend à ces sortes de poèmes. . . . Je voudrais bien savoir si la grande règle de toutes les règles n'est pas de plaire, et si une pièce de théâtre qui a attrapé son but n'a pas suivi un bon chemin.' It was easy for a popular comedian to make such a point, but it is none the less valid for that, and is perhaps the most direct aesthetic formulation of the principle on which Molière wrote. It is contradicted by two later statements, the first of which is in *L'Impromptu de Versailles*: 'L'affaire de la comédie est de représenter en général tous les défauts des hommes, et principalement des hommes de notre siècle.' The formula in the first Placet for *Tartuffe* is even sharper: 'Le devoir de la comédie étant de corriger les hommes en les divertissant.'

How are these conflicting opinions to be reconciled? Successive in time, they may convey successive reflections of a maturing artist. They may also be replies to critics. This is a vital point. In the eyes of the Church both the actor and his craft were immoral. Molière was not merely attacked on aesthetic grounds; he was called a blasphemer; his adversaries succeeded in keeping *Tartuffe* off the stage for five years and in bowdlerizing *Don Juan*. Reading the documents one cannot doubt that they wished to silence him completely. He was therefore fighting for his livelihood and for his company. 'Jamais', he wrote later, 'on ne s'était si fort déchaîné contre le théâtre.' Is it surprising that in such a struggle he should deal with the charge that the theatre was immoral, and should claim for it a power of moral correction? We should beware of accepting such statements as complete descriptions of his dramatic practice.

When we turn from the theory to the practice itself we become more than ever doubtful whether it had any moral intention. The basic fact is that the plays are full of the most lively characterizations of fools and rogues, characters which we know Molière portrayed to perfection as an actor. Surely we may assume from this that his drama is that of a *farceur* in the Gallic tradition, minus the indecency.

This *farceur* excels in bringing out contrasts and contradictions in human behaviour of the most remarkable subtlety, but he does not for that cease to be a *farceur*; his last play is farcical in much of its word and act.

The position would seem clear enough. Yet the critics will not have it. They show us a Molière who is a subjective or tragic or moral author and suggest that the comedy was merely the salting of the didactic dish. They have thus succeeded in turning the most amusing and inventive of men into a mediocre moralist, whose guiding principle is nothing more exciting than moderation in all things. It was high time for a professor of the Sorbonne to protest, as M. Mornet has recently done, that nothing in the documents justifies such an interpretation. Such facts as we do know about Molière's career suggest that he was adventurous and much more inclined to flout tradition than to respect it.

The initial error lies in confusing moral aims and moral implications. To amuse decent people, this was, as Molière once said, a strange enterprise. This he accomplished with a range and power truly marvellous, and by the force of his dramatic invention created pictures that are suggestive long after the initial shock of laughter has passed. His picture of the misanthrope and the miser and the hypochondriac have enormous implications. Implicit in them, as I hope to show, is a critique of the modern world. But it is impossible to discover that Molière had any conscious moral aim in creating them. There is strong suggestion of the contrary in the fact that great art is not produced by explicit moral intention. Let us then feel no repugnance in the investigation of the means whereby Molière evoked laughter.

It has been well said that most laughter embodies 'easily recognizable features of child's play'. This was true both of the tradition in which Molière worked and of his own practice. His characters, like children acting charades, make faces, use disguises, repetitions, echoes, and tricks which are the more amusing to those in the secret.

Then, as later, such things were found too gross by the more delicate critics:

'Et ce monsieur de la Souche, enfin, qu'on nous fait un homme d'esprit, qui paraît si sérieux en tant d'endroits, ne descend-il point dans quelque chose de trop comique et de trop outré au cinquième acte, lorsqu'il explique à Agnès la violence de son amour, avec ces roulements d'yeux extravagants, ces soupirs ridicules et ces larmes niaises qui font rire tout le monde ?'[1]

One of the attractions of this comedy for a refined society must have been its freedom from sophistication, the constant recourse to the obvious, the primitive, the elementary, which must have seemed the funnier because they tended to be despised and condemned in ordinary social behaviour. The opening situation of *Le Mariage Forcé*, for example, attains its comic effect by the elementary nature of the means employed:

'Sganarelle, parlant à ceux qui sont dans sa maison: Je suis de retour dans un moment. Que l'on ait bien soin du logis, et que tout aille comme il faut. Si l'on m'apporte de l'argent, que l'on me vienne quérir vite chez le seigneur Géronimo; et si l'on vient m'en demander, qu'on dise que je suis sorti, et que je ne dois revenir de toute la journée.'

This slight raising of the curtain of convention is the source of many comic effects. It is another significant exploitation of the mask. All of us play many parts; comedy delights in the situations that force us to abandon or interrupt the part, to remove the mask. Molière is endlessly inventing such situations, in which men get excited or angry, and cannot keep up the part. The cloak of politeness, insisted on by society, falls, to the relief of the audience because it is natural for it to do so. Trissotin, Alceste, the master of philosophy, all these start by being polite; they all end by being rude. As the polish is worn off the real man appears. The balance between nature and convention, strained in real life, is restored in the comedy. The proceeding is not always elementary. It should be studied in

[1] *Critique*, I. vii.

its superior example, the sonnet scene in *Le Misanthrope*. Alceste is too much of a gentleman to practise the sincerity he has preached. This in itself is comedy, but how much intensified when the fop annoys him and in so doing teases him back into a quite involuntary and much more natural sincerity, the plain speech of a man in a temper. Alceste's politeness and his idealism go no deeper than our own. Like us he abandons both under the most natural provocation.

Here we come upon the conflict between the living and the mechanical, out of which Bergson constructed his fascinating theory of comedy. The interplay of automatism and spontaneity is constantly shown in Molière's drama. Thibaudet once explained the success of *L'École des Femmes* by the brilliance with which this comic principle is made to conduct the action:

'*L'École des Femmes*, que l'on considère parfois comme le chef-d'œuvre de Molière, présente à l'état nu la lutte de l'automatique et du vivant, c'est-à-dire les puissances élémentaires du comique . . . plus Arnolphe plaque du mécanique sur la vie, plus la vie, par ses seules forces, fait tomber ce mécanisme, le rend inutile et incertain.'[1]

This acute criticism seems to me to penetrate into the secret of the comic art. The play referred to is not a favourite with many, on account of the improbability of its plot. For others it breathes a freshness which Molière never again achieved. The reason for this does not lie in the seriousness of its theme. Brunetière gravely demonstrates how important are the issues raised—youth, education, character—and approves the dramatic discussion of such issues. But this is to make what he calls 'une comedie à thèse' into very little more than 'une thèse de comédie' and to miss the vitality of the suggested opposition between thoughtless youth and crabbed experience. Molière did not invent this opposition, nor was he concerned to motivate it in realistic fashion. He infused it into a melodramatic scenario which he found in a short story. The plot is not the main thing at all; it merely serves to point the suggestive

[1] 'Le Rire de Molière', *Revue de Paris*, 1922, pp. 318–19.

contrast between the all-wise Arnolphe and the artless Agnès, an opposition shot through at all points with poetry and human sympathy. The high lights of the play are not the turning-points of the action; they are moments when the clash of youth and age, of spontaneity and automatism, takes shape in speech and scene. On any realistic standard of drama the Maxims of Marriage must seem a gross improbability. But how fascinating is the brittle application of principles to a living situation.[1] Is anything funnier than principles without psychology or humour, principles so austere that their formulator appears as a Mosaic lawgiver and which flatter his enormous vanity? He sees no incongruity in urging his ward to accept his grotesque vision of himself: ,

> Contemplez la bassesse où vous avez été
> Et dans le même temps admirez ma bonté.

Is not this pomposity the artistic counterpart of the letter of Agnès, that clever pastiche of awakening human desire, not yet moral at all but only natural, unacquainted with social conventions, even with those bound up in words?

'J'ai des pensées que je désirerais que vous sussiez; mais je ne sais comment faire pour vous les dire, et je me défie de mes paroles. Comme je commence à connaître qu'on m'a toujours tenue dans l'ignorance, j'ai peur de mettre quelquechose qui ne soit pas bien, et d'en dire plus que je ne devrais . . . peut-être qu'il y a du mal à dire cela; mais enfin je ne puis m'empêcher de le dire, et je voudrais que cela pût se faire sans qu'il y en eût.'

Here is no skill in expression, no experience, no *savoir-vivre*. Here is life, spontaneity, the central quality of youth unaltered and un-affected by other qualities. The comic dramatist has accomplished the marvel of dissociating social qualities from natural impulse.

Yet even this contrast is only part of the comedy, and the less dramatic part. Molière does not merely oppose artifice and *naïveté*,

---

[1] For the part played by the symbolism of the mask in this situation, cf. *supra*, p. 44.

in order to bring out the lifeless in the one and the lively in the other. He opposes them so dramatically that the lifeless is put on the defensive and, in self-defence, reacts with an animality that brings life into the inhuman and artificial. It is when Arnolphe himself falls in love, thus belying all his calculations and becoming less sinister and more ridiculous, that he comes to life, as a human being, and is himself surprised at the transformation. His scheme was to make Agnès unattractive to other men; it was a silly scheme and doomed to fail. Its failure would have corresponded to the Bergsonian theory of comedy and would have resulted in the scornful laughter of the audience at the pedant who presumed to lay a trap for youth. But Molière's comedy does not develop so and Bergson's theory explains only a part of it. Such is Arnolphe's own desire for the girl whom he had done his best to make undesirable that he revokes in one sweeping promise all the objurgations of his 'Maximes':

Tout comme tu voudras tu pourras te conduire.

Here is Gallic comedy of the raciest kind. To offer her a latch-key when he had planned that she should see no men save by his grace is to admit that he is beaten. He does not mind that because he is now eager to win her favour for himself at all costs. He has a brusque recoil of his more critical self:

Jusqu'où la passion peut-elle faire aller?

The comedy in Arnolphe is more than character-study, and I do not see that much is gained by calling it the first of the comedies of character. It is more than mockery, and exposure of the artificial and the stereotyped. It is reassuring, sympathetic, poetic in its picture of the human and the natural invading the mind of one who seemed the crassest of pedants. This is true of other plays, though rarely so transparent as in *L'École des Femmes*. The aesthetic pleasure derives from, and the dramatic invention consists in, this opposition of living and lifeless at such intensity that the artificial yields to the natural. The pose becomes unbearable and issues in the act. Both may be ridiculous; both may be ugly. Tartuffe's sensuality is perhaps as nauseating as his hypocrisy. But in his case, as in that of Arnolphe, the pose is given up, and the real man is allowed to emerge. Does not this explain why Molière's comedy can treat sinister and unattractive material and yet remain comic? On any other theory the dramatist who uses vice as comic material will seem to us to have a superficial or a warped view of vice. But neither of these epithets applies to *Tartuffe*. Evil qualities appear as evil. Nor are they pushed to one side so that we may laugh at the ridiculous accompaniments of vice. The aesthetic pleasure is much more firmly grounded, and issues in relief that we know the truth as between pose and fact. The man's nature is revealed even at the expense of his will and his plan. The angle of vision is not that of rectitude or realism but of life as opposed to all that is not alive, all that is thought or willed or assumed. The philosophical implications of this are not easy to express and must be left for a later chapter. But it may be well to take a late play that shows how much must be included in Molière's category of the comic.

The miser was one of the stock themes of comedy. Yet for comedy that explored the recesses and depths of character it was a difficult subject. The love of money is not in itself funny; it is again a vice which, if truthfully portrayed, would seem susceptible of no more than incidental humour. Furthermore, avarice is not far removed from thrift, a typical French quality. There must have been as many incipient Harpagons in a Paris audience as there were people who shared Arnolphe's views about control of the young. Yet Molière's picture is true; its popularity on the stage is proof that it is not found repulsive. We are therefore driven to ask how comedy can present avarice as refreshing. The answer is that the angle of vision is identical with that which Molière had achieved with such mastery in earlier plays. Harpagon is presented to us as a one-track man, a maniac, automatic in his endless insistence on his one standard of value. This man obsessed by money is shown in situations which do not stress, as they do not deny, his wickedness; they illumine the range and the limits of his obsession. His own energy (a significant point) drives him into situations in which he becomes a man like the rest of us. These situations often suggest Thibaudet's formulation of the Bergsonian theory: 'Le comique est plutôt raideur que laideur.' It is strange that criticism has been so slow to grasp the importance of this stiff uncompromising inhumanity, for the dramatist has been at pains to suggest it in some fullness:

'Il y a de certains esprits qu'il ne faut prendre qu'en biaisant, des tempéraments ennemis de toute résistance; des naturals rétifs, que la vérité fait cabrer, qui toujours se roidissent contre le droit chemin de la raison.' (I. v.)

The second act contains an even more explicit reference:

'Le seigneur Harpagon est de tous les humains l'humain le moins humain, le mortel de tous les mortels le plus dur et le plus serré. Il n'est point de service qui pousse sa reconnaissance jusqu'à lui faire ouvrir les mains. De la louange, de l'estime, de la bienveillance en paroles, et de l'amitié tant qu'il vous plaira; mais de l'argent, point d'affaires. Il n'est rien de plus sec et de plus aride que ses bonnes grâces et que ses caresses. . . .' (II. iv.)

The cause of this inhumanity is simply that Harpagon has transferred to money all the love and care usually given to people. As his servant goes on to say: 'il aime l'argent plus que réputation, qu'honneur et que vertu.' Harpagon sees nothing wrong with Valère's irony: 'Tout est renfermé là-dedans et *sans dot* tient lieu de beauté, de jeunesse, de naissance, d'honneur, de sagesse et de probité' (I. x). More true words are spoken in jest in Molière's work than in most drama, and the extent of Harpagon's unfeeling inhumanity is shown by his heart-felt agreement with words that to the audience convey the whole absurdity of his view. This hardness disappears only in his abject distress when he has to confess that he has loved his money and is miserable without it. These are human accents:

'Mon esprit est troublé et j'ignore où je suis, qui je suis et ce que je fais. Hélas, mon pauvre argent, mon pauvre argent, mon cher ami, on m'a privé de toi; et puisque tu m'es enlevé, j'ai perdu mon support, ma consolation, ma joie; tout est fini pour moi et je n'ai plus que faire au monde.' (IV. vii.)

This is the only play in which Molière has risked a suggestion of lunacy, and it is characteristic of his comic manner that the vital gesture of Harpagon catching at his own hand in the effort to stop the robber may be interpreted as farce, and indeed has been so by many actors. The point illustrates the extent to which the opposition of human and inhuman forces within a character has been taken. Humanity returns only in distress and in practical ruin of mental power. It implies no last-minute repentance nor softening of character. To the end Harpagon remains bitter, intractable, unteachable. But again the play is no comedy of character in the usual sense of a complete analysis of a certain type of mania. It is a study of abnormality, of the power of will and mind to make a man inhuman, together with a suggestion of the limits of that power and of the basic humanity in which every human being, even a Harpagon, is grounded. Without the ever-pervading suggestion of basic normality the play would be depressing.

It is when we get so far that we feel the Bergsonian categories to be insufficient. This is not surprising, as one should not ask of even the most brilliant theory that it exhaust the riches of a work of art. But it is difficult not to see this reminder of basic humanity as an essential part of the comic vision behind all Molière's greater plays. It is significant that neither Bergson nor Thibaudet found Tartuffe a comic character. The play is difficult to explain as a study in automatism. 'Raideur' goes only part way to explain this comedy, in which the power of the will is neutralized by the strength of appetite. A portrait of La Bruyère is perhaps of more use to us. His Télèphe is said to have been modelled on a bishop:

'Télèphe a de l'esprit, mais dix fois moins, de compte fait, qu'il ne présume d'en avoir; il est donc, dans ce qu'il dit, dans ce qu'il fait, dans ce qu'il médite et ce qu'il projette, dix fois au delà de ce qu'il a d'esprit. . . .

Il a comme une barrière qui le ferme, et qui devrait l'avertir de s'arrêter en deçà; mais il passe outre, il se jette hors de sa sphère . . . il entreprend au-dessus de son pouvoir, il désire au delà de sa portée. . . . C'est un homme qui ne se mesure point, qui ne se connaît point: son caractère est de ne savoir pas se renfermer dans celui qui lui est propre, et qui est le sien.'[1]

If this is 'raideur' it is of a fascinating and unusual kind, akin to the fanatical energy of Balzac's monomaniacs. It consists in harnessing the entire energies of the person to an objective set by mind or will without regard to the actual nature of the person. Claes, Tartuffe, Télèphe, refuse to recognize the barrier set by their own humanity to their own soaring schemes. It would be tedious to recapitulate here the features of Tartuffe's psychology (cf. *supra*, pp. 45 ff.), but in any investigation of the comedy of which it is so brilliant an example one must make clear precisely how the hypocrite has been imagined as a subject for comedy. Not, as many have thought, as satire with a coating of the ridiculous, not as a superficial view of what at close quarters would be too ugly to please; Tartuffe's wickedness is no more disguised or toned down than that of Harpagon, but the portrait, though terribly like the real thing, is not painted with a view to shock, to correct, or to warn. It is more biological than moral, displaying the strength and the limitation of a passion.

Finally, the comedy of the hypochondriac would seem to be only partly described as a case of 'raideur'. Argan has certainly given up thinking for himself and is a slave to the most idiotic statement of a doctor. He is in all this plainly comic, an autonomous person reduced to a machine: he need not be so enslaved and, in Molière's usual manner, he is pushed into positions where he gets excited and forgets the slavery. But we must also say that the comedy of *Le Malade Imaginaire* is richer than this, evident, as shown earlier (cf. *supra*, pp. 74 ff.) in Diafoirus no less than in Argan. The whole issue of the authority of the specialist is, as it were, debated and displayed

[1] *De l'Homme*, no. 141.

before us. Montaigne had raised it in terms that must have appealed to Molière. How far should we trust experts? The constitution of the human body is perhaps the most obvious case in which most of us are ignorant of facts concerning ourselves and must rely on professional experts. The French have always delighted to mock the credulity and scope for fraud that thus arises. The doctor who covers ignorance with Latin or other jargon is a stock comic figure. Molière more subtly delights to evoke the conflict between expert argument and the facts, the cases in which the expert tries to maintain his authority, even when it is his reputation and not the facts that make him do so. The thing is most neatly done perhaps in this dialogue between doctor and servant:

'Comment se porte son cocher? — Fort bien, il est mort. — Mort? — Oui. — Cela ne se peut. — Je ne sais pas si cela se peut, mais je sais bien que cela est. — Cela est impossible. Hippocrate dit . . . — Hippocrate dira ce qu'il lui plaira, mais le cocher est mort. — (Sganarelle) Paix, discoureuse.' (*Amour Médecin*, sc. ii.)

The comic sting of the last word lies in the fact that it is not the maid who is fabricating 'discours' but the doctor. Out of respect for the doctor the master has to tell the maid not to argue.

In all this Molière was certainly renewing an old French theme. But he was no less working on a typical modern problem. The complexity of civilization has narrowed so surprisingly the area in which we can make up our own minds on the facts (witness the car-driver ignorant of mechanics) that the question of confidence in experts has for the twentieth century even more topicality than it had for the seventeenth. Molière's audience could not feel, as we feel, that they were at the parting of the ways, that the immense advance of science was to make every man accept more and more in the way of technicalities. Mechanical jargon is now supreme and uncontrollable in large areas of our daily life.

Any discussion of Molière's comedy must deal with its profundity and subtlety, and tends to obscure the fact that it set out to be neither. In much of its incident, and in form, it is elemental and primary, exploiting the eternal themes of comic emotion. Indeed its strength and appeal lie in the fact that it is less a creation of ingenuity than a return to well-known human situations. No account of it should fail to show how it exploits the basic comic feature of surprise. 'Laughter', said Hobbes, 'is sudden glory. Both laughter and weeping are sudden motions, custom taking them both away.' This joy of being taken by surprise, off one's guard, without time for reflection, is one of the delights of watching or even reading Molière. 'L'effet est admirable', as Don Juan said when Sganarelle praised the virtues of 'le vin émétique' that worked such marvels that it was given to a dying man, and he died.

Closely allied to this element of surprise is that of naïve vanity painfully reaching an obvious and flat conclusion. Jourdain, after engaging expensive teachers, discovers that 'tout ce qui est prose n'est point vers, et tout ce qui n'est point vers est prose', and adds the delightful reflection: 'Heu, voilà ce que c'est que d'étudier.' The joy and surprise of coming upon these banalities derive from the fact that Jourdain's statement is true and that he has no idea of the fact. That is, precisely, what he has gained by study. In similar vein are the comments of authors on their own bad poetry. Trissotin and Oronte, though delightful, are no improvement upon Mascarille: 'Avez-vous remarqué ce commencement, "Oh, Oh", voilà qui est extraordinaire, "Oh, Oh", comme un homme qui s'avise tout d'un coup, "Oh, Oh".'

Sometimes in a serious passage Molière will attain what seems to be the perfect image of the inane. The self-satisfied Marquis Acaste, for example, solemnly recounts his excellent qualities of manner, bearing, mind, and social position. His speech may be read as a satiric sketch of the idle rich by a hard-working bourgeois, but it achieves a singular purity of comedy by its complete absence of any modesty or self-criticism. As the latest editor of the play has said: 'De voir un être aussi totalement entiché de lui-même que l'est

Acaste vous met dans une joie qui touche à la béatitude. Il désarme; point de résistance chez le spectateur, ni de moralité, ni de classe; une satisfaction parfaite, une satisfaction d'artiste, qu'un homme remplisse aussi absolument sa définition.'[1]

Such perfection admits of no easy analysis. One may discern as present within it a blend of the elemental, the bland, and the inane, together with a critical, realist view of men and the world. Indeed, the critical and the artistic seem to meet in such comic types as Acaste or Jourdain. They are as far from sheer intellectual mockery as they are from sentiment. They do not invariably arouse laughter, but the laughter is never extraneous to the essential features. It would seem to be, as laughter probably physiologically is, a physical irruption of the emotion caused by comic juxtaposition. We do not laugh much at the main scenes of *Tartuffe* and *Le Misanthrope*, but the comedy is none the less present. These sombre portraits are at one end of a comic scale that includes the elementally absurd, the automatic, the lunatic, and the lover. Perhaps the one element common to the entire scale is the basic emphasis on nature. Every play shows in some form how nature is flouted and will return, how the most violently upset balance will at moments be righted. Every play is a study of abnormality, with an assumption and background of normality, not of social behaviour but of natural constitution. 'Toute comédie de Molière est à la fois une danse et une démonstration.' We are shown, at the same time as the mime, a proof that men are men, however much they may try to make themselves supermen or may be degraded to sub-human servility. When the mime is over and Tartuffe and Harpagon have left the boards, we do not feel anger against the Church or the rich, our sense of justice or morality is not outraged or enflamed, we feel enlightened, reassured because we know; we know the facts, the basic facts, we know the nature of these puppets who tried to conceal or to force their nature; we understand.

[1] *Le Misanthrope*, ed. Rudler, p. xxxii.

VIII. STAGE

THE final stages of the argument of the last chapter suggest that we must seek for a new content to what has been called 'the moral teaching of Molière'. It is doubtful indeed whether we are justified in using such an expression at all. Molière never claimed to be a teacher. The primary business of comedy is not to instruct. The stage is something else before it is a pulpit. The attempt to find moral lessons in the plays brought even that astute critic Émile Faguet to the verge of absurdity. All such inquiries savour of the schoolboy's question as to what *Paradise Lost* was meant to prove. They are a pedantic irrelevance which would have afforded rich enjoyment to the master of comedy whose work they obscure. There is no more need to extract the moral lesson of *L'Avare* than that of *Othello*. Both works stand or fall, not as illustrations of any precept, or even of any single idea, but as embodying an artistic vision, as creations of art.

It is indeed surprising that this point has to be made in connexion with Molière, the most unintellectual of dramatists. His artistic medium made no pretensions to profundity as usually understood. It aimed at effects of laughter, amusement, surprise, which are effects more immediate, less intellectual, than those of reflection, meditation, homily. Except in the heat of controversy he never claimed to be other than a *farceur* whose intention was to please and amuse 'decent people'.

Yet this in itself, as he once admitted, was a 'strange enterprise'.

Strange perhaps because it involved antagonizing powerful people and interests, and further because in execution it involved a constant change of tone and lightness of touch. Nothing could be systematic or profound or realistic for long, for any longer than it was fascinating or amusing. All this, as previous chapters have attempted to show, makes the peculiar aesthetic of comedy; it makes generalization about the moral elements in comedy a risky proceeding. I do not see how one can speak of the philosophy of a man who on principle never declared it, who concealed his own views so successfully behind his dramatic creations that critics determined to discover doctrine have only succeeded in extracting the dullest and flattest of principles from comedy that is never dull and never flat. 'La parfaite raison fuit toute extrémité': this is held up as the guiding principle of a play full of poetry and comedy. But the banality of the principle and the invention of the comedy are so entirely incompatible that the principle must be abandoned.

But if, as suggested in these pages, we give less attention to the intentions of this drama, and more to its intensity, our difficulties vanish. These vivid dramatic creations become, not illustrations of propositions, but creations of the imagination. And at once they become significant, by their variety, psychology, and most of all by the fantasy which in most of them seems to achieve a compound of realism and unreality, so that they have, and give, the illusion of life inseparable from the pleasures of art. If we are to penetrate into the mind of their creator it is this world of fantasy that we must watch, bewaring all the time of constructing theories that do not accord with its facts.

'La vision comique souligne le désaccord entre la raison et la vie.' This short phrase of M. Fernandez suggests such a new approach. Molière's fantasy delights apparently to produce situations in which constructions of the mind are opposed to act and fact. M. Jourdain's fencing-master is so eloquent as to convince him 'qu'on peut tuer un homme par raison démonstrative'; the phrase is a delicious juxtaposition of opposing spheres. The master of philosophy argues brilliantly about the evil of losing one's temper ... and straightway loses his. Much more serious, but embedded in a play where the prevailing tone is one of farce, is the position of Dandin, who is in the right and is constantly made to appear in the wrong: 'J'enrage d'avoir tort lorsque j'ai raison.' The logical end, in our world, of exasperation such as his would be suicide. Molière's comedy ends with this thought: 'Le meilleur parti qu'on puisse prendre c'est de s'aller jeter dans l'eau, la tête la première.'

This example is worth a moment's pause. The tone is of the lightest and in the traditional view we should not draw conclusions from what is obviously 'not serious'. We here touch the nerve, perhaps, of the sterility of much Molière criticism. The so-called 'seriousness' of the dramatist's tone does not affect his intellectual point. It is, quite literally, 'beside the point' to inquire whether we are meant to take seriously Dandin's threat to kill himself. The whole situation is farcical, because he is such a silly man. But the intellectual point of his dilemma is quite independent of this. Even a silly man may suggest the difference between the world of the mind and the world of fact. And in comedy, as in other forms of poetry, suggestion is enough.

Suggestion is all that is possible in comedy in which the absurd is admitted and even welcomed. What is more absurd than the whole setting of *Amphitryon*? Yet the absurdity is a game played to the entertainment of the intellect, from the rigorous logic of which it sets us for a moment free. Mercury taking the form of Sosie succeeds in persuading him that he is not himself. Since he knows things that only Sosie could know, he must, according to the evidence, be right. Even identity must yield to evidence:

> Il a raison. A moins d'être Sosie
> On ne peut pas savoir tout ce qu'il dit ...
>
> Il ne ment pas d'un mot, à chaque repartie,
> Et de moy je commence à douter tout de bon.

Près de moy, par la force, il est déjà Sosie:
Il pourroit bien encore l'estre, par la raison.
Pourtant quand je me tâte, et que je me rapelle,
Il me semble que je suis moy. (485)

The joke is that, although absurd, these things *are*:

                    la chose à chacun
          Hors de créance doit paroistre;
          C'est un fait à n'y rien connoistre,
          Un conte extravagant, ridicule, importun;
          Cela choque le sens commun
          Mais cela ne laisse pas d'estre. (771)

But this play offers only one extreme form of the interplay between life and mind. Others have been adduced in previous chapters. Arnolphe's scheming, perfect on paper, is exposed by the
reality. No less so is that of Tartuffe, whose plan was perfect,
except in its miscalculation of his own make-up. We have seen how
Argan's plight results from confusing jargon, invented mystification, with statement of fact. Purgon's curses, invented to terrify
him, do so because he takes them as actual descriptions of what will
happen to him. Béralde points the distinction: 'Ce qu'il dit, que
fait-il à la chose?'

If Molière be justly called a poet, we shall expect to find this distinction between mind and life in situations that are more than
amusing. To get things wrong, to miscalculate, is after all an ancient
theme of comedy. But the case of Dandin is surely more suggestive
than this. He does not merely miscalculate; in so far as he does, he
is himself to blame for having married the wrong woman; in him
Molière renews the butt of the old comedy. But alongside this there
is the continuing suggestion, no more, that it is possible to be right
and wrong about things at the same time. It is a suggestion of a
philosophical nature, concerning the difference between essence
and accident. Dandin is essentially in the right, but he is in all
actual cases made to appear in the wrong. He complains of this with

energy and determines to prove himself, as well as to be, in the right: 'J'ai eu beau voir et beau dire, votre adresse l'a toujours emporté sur mon bon droit, et toujours vous avez trouvé moyen d'avoir raison; mais à cette fois, Dieu merci, les choses vont être éclaircies, et votre effronterie sera pleinement confondue.' But this does not happen and the suggestion is that things cannot be arranged to support even the best case. 'J'admire mon malheur'; Dandin gets no farther than stupefaction at the incongruous ways of the world.

But in this respect Dandin is but a hasty sketch beside the finished prototype of Alceste. He, too, is convinced that he is right; he has right on his side, but not the law. His anger that the law should not in fact do what it is supposed to do and convict the man who is in the wrong, what is this but another case of argument, conviction, idea on the one side, and the facts, reality, the event on the other? Some of Molière's finest passages arraign the perversity of the world:

> Trop de perversité règne au siècle où nous sommes
> Et je veux me tirer du commerce des hommes.
> Quoi, contre ma partie on voit tout à la fois
> L'honneur, la probité, la pudeur et les lois;
> On publie en tous lieux l'équité de ma cause;
> Sur la foi de mon droit mon âme se repose;
> Cependant je me vois trompé par le succès:
> J'ai pour moi la justice et je perds mon procès.

To this feature of Molière's greatest dramatic character we shall return, but for the moment one may use its concordance with characters in other plays to show how different is Molière's stage from the world of which it seems to be a faithful reproduction. In his drama life is ordered and worked into a pattern. The dramatic situations seem frequently to proceed from a sense of the gap between what is within the mind and what is outside it. Human energies, of intellect, will, passion, cunning, learning, power, are opposed to natural forces in themselves, in others, in things, which they disregard and are apt to discount until they are brought up sharply against them by circumstance. This circumstance is, of course, always manipulated by the dramatist, and so the situations have meaning, they are the fruit of his own judgement on the vast discrepancy of life. The poet's mind, says M. Fernandez again, 'substitue au désordre de la vie l'ordre d'une réflexion qui rassemble de multiples observations éparses. L'événement n'obéit plus aux lois de la vie, tout en conservant les apparences, mais aux lois de la raison.'[1] If this be so, we must look in the texture of the plays for the mind of the author, but not to the views expressed by any one character, for we dare not identify one creation out of many with the mind that has created them all. We shall look rather at the general nature and scope of the situations as presented to us. If they show up the fallibility of human judgements, then we are watching the play of Molière's own judgement upon human judgement as he sees it.

Here we return to the mask, which in a previous chapter was suggested as the principle and symbol of Molière's comedy. It is the symbol of the automatic, the fictitious, imposed upon the living and the real. At first sight this would seem to imply a judgement upon life that would render great art impossible. The critical attitude, anxious to exploit any and every deviation from the normal, might make a miser seem ridiculous and might create amusement in a bourgeois audience by caricaturing a bourgeois aping the gentry. But it would not go far to account for such astonishingly human creations as Harpagon and Jourdain. Are we not driven to the conclusion that the critical attitude in Molière is not primary but derivative, resting on a sounder, saner, and more positive conception of human nature? Do not the contrasts pointed out in this chapter suggest what this is? It might be rash to define it by any single epithet. It has been called respect for nature, which has led to misinterpretation. Molière exhibits the limits of human nature no less than its powers. It apparently implies a sober

[1] For the full quotation, see p. 25 above.

sense of man's place in nature, of his function, of that order and sobriety to overstep which is to be unnatural. On such a basis are all his pictures of abnormality constructed, the most imposing collection of fools and rogues imagined by any dramatist. Yet they are not remarkable and interesting only as embodying the abnormal, but as illustrating the normal in themselves. Here lies frequently the comedy: the natively human, like a rubber spring, constantly jumps back and shifts the mask of superstition or pedantry or snobbery or avarice. In this contest of mask and face, of wit and nature, of mind against life, let us not ask who wins. The comedy does not determine the relative strength of the forces pitted against each other; it illustrates, in bewildering variety, their juxtaposition and coexistence.

To those who know the French tradition this vision will come as no new thing, although unique in power and range. It has been well said that on many points Rousseau is at one with Molière in his criticism of society. The satire of Voltaire has the same broad appreciation of the powers and limits of human nature. Though documentary evidence is not to be had, it is fairly certain that Molière learnt much from at least two of his predecessors. Of Rabelais it has been said that 'il fit la guerre à tout ce qui dans la religion, la science et la société est contraire à la nature et à la raison, s'éleva contre la pédanterie, l'ascétisme et la superstition; à l'antiphysie il oppose Physis, qui "enfanta Beauté et Harmonie" '.[1] In the work of Montaigne Molière could find many of his main themes explicit. He must surely have read the mordant satire against doctors, religious hypocrites ('Je ne trouve aucune qualité si aisée à contrefaire que la dévotion'), against the presumption that accompanies learning, the mask imposed by social behaviour and the effects of 'imagination'. Montaigne was aware of the distinction between natural and acquired faculties; he was alive to the gulf that separates concepts from objects: 'Nous disons bien Puissance, Vérité, Justice,

[1] Vedel, op. cit., p. 313.

paroles qui signifient quelquechose de grand, mais cette chose-là nous ne la voyons aucunement.' Above all he taught that attempts to improve on nature usually lead away from nature: 'La peste de l'homme est l'opinion de science ... O cuider, combien tu nous empesches.' Those who try to be clever, who think themselves advanced or superior or wise, are the more ridiculous: 'Nos folies ne me font pas rire, ce sont nos sagesses.'

While exploring the affinities of Molière's attitude, let us not forget that Shakespeare also was in the Renaissance tradition. He, too, sought comedy in the fictions of the brain, exposed (or better, exploded) by the event. In George Gordon's happy phrase, what is set up in the pride of fancy he delights to undermine with the pride of life.[1] Such a distinction between the fanciful and the real has at least two features in common with Molière's view. It rests on a similar concept of natural equilibrium, and it implies in the angle of vision a quality which can only be called serenity. It is difficult to explain otherwise why we find Dogberry and Benedict and Jourdain and Sganarelle refreshing figures. It has been said that we do not take them seriously, that their foibles are of no great consequence. But the real explanation covers Tartuffe and Harpagon as well: though vicious they are imagined with sympathy and serenity that discerns, not any goodness which an idealist might wish to see in them, but the humanity that accompanies their vice and renders them akin to all of us.

A marked feature of what we have called Molière's world is the acceptance of society as the natural ground in which human qualities grow. This might seem a necessary accompaniment of drama, portraying as it does the actions and reactions of people. But it is none the less remarkable that Molière has so sharply criticized features of the actual society in which he worked, while never denying that social relationship is the touchstone of human behaviour. The effect of assuming a mask, whether of roguery, pedantry, or fear, is to

[1] *Shakespearian Comedy*, p. 14.

separate the wearer from his fellows, to put him on another plane, to isolate him. This social reference is much stronger in Molière's comedy than in Shakespeare. The distress of Hamlet is human, cosmic, moral; that of Harpagon is moral and social. Money sunders him from human relations. Characteristically, he makes the point himself, to his children:

> 'Cela est étrange, que mes propres enfants me trahissent et deviennent mes ennemis.

CLÉANTE: Est-ce être votre ennemi que de dire que vous avez du bien?
HARPAGON: Oui. De pareils discours, et les dépenses que vous faites, seront cause qu'un de ces jours on viendra chez moi me couper la gorge.'

In the later stages of his mania he sees no one who does not give him cause for suspicion: 'Qui soupçonnez-vous de ce vol? — Tout le monde.'

The aesthetic of this attitude is worth some attention. Molière is here again in line with the French tradition and attitude. 'The most fruitful exercise of the mind, to my thinking,' said Montaigne, 'is intercourse with others.' It is, therefore, natural to find French comedy seeking its subject in those forces which sunder men from such intercourse, to find subject for criticism and amusement in the crank, the exception, especially in the man whose vanity causes him to set himself apart and above his fellows. Distinction of mind and brain is not in the French view worth separation from those less gifted. 'Un homme d'esprit serait souvent embarrassé sans la compagnie des sots.' Molière would seem to take the same view as La Rochefoucauld. His Don Juan is comic in that he thinks himself self-sufficient and constantly needs and enjoys the company of the valet whom intellectually he despises. And the aesthetic result of such pictures, upon an audience who share this view, is again liberation and reassurance, as the poet unravels before them the strength and legitimacy of the social bond. Many instances could be taken, grave and gay, but the peak of achievement, in this as in so many

respects, is *Le Misanthrope*. The subject of this play is society; its
butt is anti-social, individual to the point of renouncing contact
with his fellows. The man of honour, whose high principle makes
it impossible to go on living with the rest of the world—it is perhaps
hard for those of us who are not French to realize how rich a subject
of comedy this is in Paris. We tend to see in this subject a rather
cynical admission that the reformer is always in the wrong and that
society and habit will stifle individual conscience. But the setting is
more subtle. Alceste is ridiculous, in a fine sense, not because he
rebukes the society of his day of insincerity. I think it could be
shown that his honesty in doing so is not made to appear anything
other than admirable. He is ridiculous because he forgets that he is
part of the picture. He is anti-social because he recommends on
grounds of principle courses of action by which he stands to gain.
It is one thing to reprove flattery and flirtation; it is quite another to
insist that one be preferred to all other suitors. Alceste has no sense
of this distinction. He brooks no rivals: 'De tout l'univers vous
devenez jaloux.' This is true, and comparable to Harpagon's isola-
tion. But whereas Harpagon is a symbol of absorption and slavery
to a commodity, Alceste is a symbol of something much more
interesting and complicated.

In order to bring out the range and depth of Molière's character-
ization, it is worth while trying to see what this elusive quality is.
One might call it the confusion of the general and the personal. It is
a natural human tendency to cover and defend one's actions by the
appeal to a standard outside oneself. Conversely, we often fail to see
how much our adherence to such a general standard is a consequence
of self-interest and vanity. A prominent member of a church choir
will presumably account for his activity by claiming that he is
anxious to contribute to worship. What he does not say, and may
not even realize, is that he may also be obeying deep urges of display
and exhibition that are active in his subconscious self. Since Freud
we have had to admit the subconscious as a determinant of human

behaviour. But before Freud artists have shown it at work. 'Je veux qu'on me distingue', says Alceste, meaning by the first person little more than the indeterminate 'on', and making the quite valid point that protestations of friendship should be kept for cases in which the friendship is really felt and not uttered as a meaningless social formula. But we know how any reformer tends to identify himself with his cause and unconsciously to become a pattern. This is implied in the effort to 'live up to one's principles', as we say. And what Alceste wanted, unbeknown to himself, was recognition, preference, distinction. His admirably ambiguous phrase means much more than he consciously meant by it. But that is comic language as we have discussed it in an earlier chapter and as only Molière can use it. It corresponds to the attitude of the comic poet who sees the ambiguity of all human profession.

Would it be thought too far-fetched to trace this attitude in a different sphere, that of politics? The politician must relate events and policies to principles, if he is to obtain assent for them. In his view and suggestion assent to the principles implies assent to the policies. Thus in stirring his people to continue an exhausting war he will say that Justice comes before Peace. If he is trying to prevent the nation taking up arms, he will say the opposite: Peace comes first, even before Justice. A political writer has recently analysed utterances of twentieth-century statesmen and quoted some damaging cases of the habit, to which Anglo-Saxons seem especially prone, of thus confusing the particular with the general. Theodore Roosevelt, for example, on one occasion said: 'These are American principles ... they are the principles of mankind and must prevail.'[1] Of all such confusions Alceste is the poetic prototype, not conceived to further any way of thinking, but in its range applicable to the curious mixture of conscious and sub-conscious in any outspoken social attitude.

It would of course be quite false to think of *Le Misanthrope* as a

[1] Cit. E. H. Carr, *The Twenty Years' Crisis*, pp. 81–112.

play about politics. Molière knew nothing about politics in our sense and certainly had no intention of treating any such serious issue. His only intention as far as we know (the point has been so often neglected that it must be repeated) was to amuse. But, in the process of dramatizing his theme of the misanthropic lover, the intensity of his creative power has led him to sketch a figure far beyond any intention and comparable to Hamlet in its wide range of suggestion, personal, social, ethical, political, even theological. The type of Alceste occurs in all these contexts; it is a type peculiar to the modern world, to which the thought of Montaigne may well have introduced Molière, the world in which truth is not indubitably revealed but claimed by conflicting parties. The reformer with the best case in the world cannot 'get it across' except in the partial issues of actual conflicts. If he contents himself with laying down principles and expects the world to adopt them in actual situations, conditioned as those situations will be by personal forces, then like Alceste he will lose heart and temper, and may well take refuge in an ivory tower of disgust, grimly pleased to find that the world is as bad as he always said it was.

Such are some of the issues raised by Molière's most elusive play. Those issues cannot be discerned as long as one looks for the author's view behind the words of this or that character. The author's view (if this be the right expression) is in the all-embracing conception of a situation in which all characters of his play are set. It is that conception which animates the mime and which is the first cause of our enjoyment.

CONCLUSION

THE foregoing chapters contain a considerable amount of repetition, a feature difficult to avoid when the inquiry is conducted on methodological rather than on chronological or departmental lines. Treatment of the mask, for example, needs for adequate illustration some of the material used in the chapter on language. That is one more reason for not summing up the inquiry by tiresome recapitulation of points already made perhaps too obvious. On the other hand, the reader who has followed the steps is entitled to ask where they lead and what, if any, are the positions justified by the argument. Is he not also entitled to some answer to the question whether these finicking distinctions do not mean the reading of an alien subtlety into plain seventeenth-century fun-making? If asked whether Molière were conscious of the implications of his irony or of the complexities which we have tried to analyse, one might well say that he very probably was not. But the present concern is not with Molière's motives, nor with his intentions, in the first place. The concern is with his work in the form in which he left it. That work has exerted, and continues to exert, a singular power over both players and public. I suggest that the cause of that power is to be found in its subtlety, in its profundity, in its magnificently instinctive (and no doubt unconscious) sense of comedy. It is in the detailed analysis that pedantic arguments emerge; they must not be imputed to the maker of the comedy.

The sequence of chapters will, I hope, already have suggested why consideration of the actor should lead all the others. The germ of the play is the 'jeu de scène' which Molière learnt from the Italians. This was the feature in which he first showed his mastery, the by-play or grimace or deception that is the kernel of any single scene. One could hardly call this a literary feature. It becomes literary only when broadcast, so to speak, to a larger public than can crowd into the theatre. In origin it is a physical expression of some human attitude, and here our study of the comedy must begin, for we can trace it no farther back.

Where does the actor himself begin? With the mask, or affixed character, behind which he hides, out of which he pops, into which he returns. This was the stock-in-trade of the popular French theatre. It depended on cases of confused identity, people taken for other people, posing as other people. Molière's first Parisian farce bears all the marks of his mature comedy: the girls are deceived by the masked servants and themselves don the mask of culture. The masters, in a single farcical gesture, expose both servants and girls as frauds. This rigidity of character or profession which marks the doctor, the hypocrite, the blue-stocking, and the miser is by dramatic action exposed and expelled to show the natural gross humanity which lies much deeper than all profession.

To represent all this, two means were open: dumb show, ballet, gesture, grimace on the one hand, speech on the other. Neither is neglected, but the use of speech enforces the irony already partly perceptible in the situation. To watch Arnolphe bar the door and glare at his ward is one thing; to hear him muttering how strange it is that folk are so pig-headed, that is quite another, and a new form of dramatic irony. Molière's drama would lose its major animation without the eternal ricochet of repartee and contradiction that links its actors to their action. But the language does no more than externalize, with extreme subtlety, the ambiguities of the situation. We need not think of two men, one creating the action and the other fitting the words: drama is not opera. Act and word suggest a common origin, in the ironic conception of human behaviour.

Such are the forces which seem to be active in the invention of a single scene. But even the slightest comedies contain several scenes and most of them several acts. The inquiry must therefore deal with the grouping of scenes and the method whereby the impression of a single dramatic encounter is repeated, prolonged, developed. None of the usual explanations of Molière's dramatic structure does as a matter of fact explain the architecture of his plays. To consider them as character studies, or as plots in the usual sense, or as social satires, is to leave certain successful parts of each play unaccounted for. There is no reason why some scenes should not be episodic in this way; the seventeenth-century audience may have liked as much as its modern counterpart does the 'extra' funny scene tacked on to the main subject of the play. Our examination of the structure of one or two of the greater plays, however, has suggested a technique of suffusion, or of progressive illumination of a central idea. Alain and Georgette do not fit into a character study of Arnolphe, nor into the plot of 'the useless precaution'; they do animate a discussion of the contrast between *naïveté* and sophistication. Arsinoé has little to do with the portrait of an idealist, but she has everything to do with the portrait of the implications and modes of sincerity.

Such considerations may help us to see something of the working of the comic machine. We must beware of thinking that they explain the dramatic creation. That is something not to be explained; it remains a mystery which we must approach with proper caution, mindful that our first observations may savour of paradox. For many people it is hardly right to speak of Molière's work as creation at all. They find it difficult to believe that so exact an imitation of human behaviour has been created; it seems to them the result of observation and not of imagination. How are we to reconcile this with the view that finds both situations and characters unreal and improbable? Hazlitt, for example, cannot find epithets strong enough to express his dislike: the comedies are 'laboured', improbable, extravagant. The *Misanthrope* is absurd. 'The improbability of the character of Orgon is wonderful.' Which view must we adopt?

The difficulties begin to clear if we ask more strictly what is meant by the epithets. Do those who find the portraits realistic mean any more than 'lifelike'? Are they thinking of the policy of Tartuffe, or of natural speech and gesture? The latter is indeed drawn to the life; character is, as a contemporary said, 'observé avec une exactitude qui avait été jusque-là inconnue sur le théâtre de Paris'. The situations, on the other hand, have every kind of improbability: they are grotesque, exaggerated, lacking in psychology; if taken seriously, they fail to convince. Yet who notices these improbabilities during the performance? Are we the less interested in Tartuffe because Orgon is too easy a prey? In Argan because he seems at times to overstep the limit of gullibility? In Harpagon because such a person would not be likely to flatter a girl?

It may be English prejudice that induces us to judge drama on a standard of realism. Why not face the fact that the procedure is farcical, in the manner of the sketch in the modern musical comedy? Close study compels us indeed to say more than this. The distinctive feature is seen to be neither realism nor unreality, but a constant veering from one to the other. Within a scene the tone will change from banter to serious discussion. The actors behave naturally in unnatural situations; the keynote is variety. Professor Mornet's observation on the subject of *George Dandin* applies to other plays: '*George Dandin* nous met plus ou moins dans une atmosphère de farce, mais il suffirait de hausser toute la pièce d'un ton pour qu'elle devienne une comédie grave, et de deux pour qu'elle devienne une tragédie . . . la fantaisie touche parfois à la farce pour revenir ensuite vers la vérité.'[1]

[1] *Histoire de la littérature française classique*, pp. 262–3.

This lightness of touch is perhaps the key to the appreciation of other beauties in this drama. M. Jouvet's phrase about Molière's denouements is of wider application: 'Ils sont de la plus fine convention théâtrale.' We gain nothing by putting so mercurial a showman in a straitjacket and asking him to be either grave or gay. His muse, for we are in the realm of poetry, is distinguished precisely by the ease with which subjects and tones change under our gaze. The only standard constantly observed is what has been called 'l'optique du théâtre', that is, what can be made to pass as living and active at the moment of representation. The momentary flashing into life, such is the key to the technique. It makes the comedy somewhat akin to the modern short story: no explanations, no careful preparation, no realistic following-out of the consequences. The act, for the moment, is real; we see people in action; we receive the suggestion, and no more, of life. This may well seem superficial to those who want things accounted for and explained. Hazlitt is clearly and ponderously right in declaring Orgon improbable. But is it possible to miss the point more completely? The credibility of Orgon interests the dramatist only so far as Orgon confronts us in action. After that the puppet has served his turn and may be put back in the box. But let us note two features that Hazlitt could equally well have seen had he been interested. First of all, there is no waiting in these plays. Something happens all the time; the mind of the spectator is occupied, if he will only take what is offered and not ask for something else. Secondly, the kaleidoscope has a theme; as they flit past, like the shots of a film, the gestures make up an impression and an attitude. The lover of Molière's plays finds them easier to grasp and more delightful to watch because of this very mixture of real and unreal in swift procession. He is accessible to the fantasy and to the poetry.

For is it not of poetry that we must speak? If we try to analyse what sort of a quality animates the show and relates mime to jest and jest to scene, observation will not do as answer. We are driven to

suppose that kind of invention which is the prerogative of poetry.
These puppets cannot have been merely observed, for no men are so
active or so charming as they are. What delights us in the plays is
the constant appearance of

> Such shaping fantasies that apprehend
> More than cool reason comprehends.

Farce, said Claudel once, is lyrical in its sublimity, and anyone who
has watched *Le Bourgeois Gentilhomme* unfold before him will know
what is meant. One could observe a fop or a gullible bourgeois, but
what observation would make his music teacher say:

Et si tous les hommes apprenaient la musique, ne serait-ce pas le
moyen de s'accorder ensemble, et de voir dans le monde la paix
universelle?

A first characteristic of this quality is its energy. It has been well
said that these characters, like their creator, 'have quicksilver in
their veins'.[1] The plays are full of restless vigour; the scenes are
constructed on the assumption that if only he can be whipped into
activity the impostor will show his true colours, the pedant will forget his jargon, and the social man his code.

No less remarkable than the energy is the freedom to change the
tone, to be grave and gay at once, farcical and serious, nonsensical
and reasonable. The play just referred to, *George Dandin*, is an
excellent example of this fantastic liberty.[2] It is based on the crudest
conventions of the old farce. Its hero is 'le mari confondu', shut
out of his own front door, forced like a naughty boy to apologize to
his penniless but noble father-in-law. The man let into the secret is
just the wrong man. These hard-worked devices are the seventeenth-
century counterparts of the nondescript film. Yet the tone varies
from crudity to serious reflection and is at times suggestive of deep
conflicts quite other than the gross gestures on the stage. The
naïveté of the cheated husband is not in the usual story, nor his
obstinate search for the truth, nor his touching persuasion that he is

[1] Cf. *supra*, p. 38.   [2] Cf. *supra*, pp. 118–19.

right. His pathetic monologues suggest (and do no more than suggest) the gulf between being right and making other people admit you are right: 'J'admire mon malheur . . . est-il possible que les apparences toujours tourneront contre moi?' This is neither sentimental nor serious: it is the fantasy of comedy.

This fantasy makes Molière's comedy unique in its combination of the grave and the gay. The plays impart a kind of mock seriousness in their teasing mixture of comic tones, which leave a subject in the mind as mere suggestion; one may take it or leave it. This comedy is more adaptable than any other. 'Molière est admirable en ceci que la matière qu'il offre à ses interprètes est éminemment plastique, je veux dire pétrissable et qu'on en fait à peu près tout ce que l'on veut.' One has only to consider the cases where different interpretations have been equally successful. Tartuffe has been played as a glutton and as a delicate philanderer. The lunacy of Harpagon is tragic, and farcical. What nuances cannot be read into Alceste? A recent performance of *Le Malade Imaginaire* made the most of the farcical setting, whereas others have suggested the more serious themes of the play.

The implications of drama such as this are enormous, but it is risky to speak of its intention, or of the thought behind it. Those who have claimed to arrive at what they call 'le fond de la pensée' of the author have not contributed much to the elucidation of his work. For the master of irony eludes; it is his business to be elusive, for he of all artists has the power to combine sympathy and criticism. We may not be able to say with any certainty what Molière thought about religion or nature or marriage. What his work allows us to say is that he was the kind of poet who can imagine men clinging to pretensions, greedy for power, blind to others' interests, deluding themselves, hoaxing their fellows. All this he has imagined and portrayed to the life. And around such men he has raised storms of banter and arrays of traps, so that they may be cheated of their desire and exposed in their folly. Yet this mad chase of folly and 'follies' is never unaccompanied by sympathy, fellow feeling, the humanity of the true artist. The rogues and fools are not less but more likeable when exposed or baited. They seem more natural and more human; even the hideous afford a glimpse of humanity.

Here is irony in its full power, defying all but the most delicate analysis. It may be that the stress laid in these pages on imagination seems to do less than justice to the qualities of the intellect. As M. Fernandez reminds us, 'le rire est une émotion de la raison'. Molière's laughter is, like that of Meredith, 'the laughter of reason refreshed'. The judgement of the author is never absent from the work. That judgement, that assessment of intellectual forces, is perhaps the salt to which comedy owes its savour. Arnolphe laughed to hear the simplicities of Agnès, but our enjoyment is greater than his, for we have not (in the theatre at least) his limiting sense of superiority. We read the famous letter rejoicing not only in its *naïveté* but in the ironic power of vision and style that produced so true a picture of *naïveté*. André Gide warned his friends not to listen solely to Hermione, but in the accents of Hermione to hear the poet Racine. So in enjoying Molière let us not fail to recognize what we may be unable adequately to define. Perhaps if we were to continue the search for a master quality, one that would include the laughter, the cool judgement, the social sense, the equanimity, and the sympathy, we could surmise no more of the poet's mind than to say of him what George Sand said of Balzac: 'Son âme était d'une grande sérénité.'

POSTSCRIPT

THE best way to test a teacher's views is to try them on plenty of students. This I have done, with the substance of the preceding chapters. Thanks to their uninhibited reactions, I have come to see more clearly both the nature and the limits of what I was trying to express in 1949.

It still seems to me quite wrong to begin with Molière the man. The facts do not allow us to say anything valid about his life, or his ideas. How he lived, what he read, what were his relations with women—about all these things we really know very little. Molière the man is in fact a shadowy character. The books that claim to tell us about him admit that they are reduced to conjecture. It has been recently claimed that scepticism as to his life has gone too far: 'on est allé trop loin dans les négations'. Maybe, but let us leave this delicate assessment of what can be said for certain and what can be only guessed at to those who have time for it. The important thing about Molière is the work that he has left to us. This can be scientifically studied, and may in the end give us clues about the man and his mind. But those come only after long study; the right place to begin study is the plays themselves. If students only realized this—in itself not a very difficult point—they would save themselves much floundering and obtain increased enjoyment. Enjoyment is after all what the plays aimed to provide, and what they have provided for generations of playgoers and students.

To start with, then, we can know many things about how and

when and for whom the plays were written. We can, and should, know that Molière's work is not literature at all in the usual sense: it is drama written to be acted rather than read, written in haste and not in cloistered ease, written for money rather than for its author's pleasure in self-expression.

To know so much is to be free to look for new elements in the plays, dramatic elements for instance, points of structure that enlarge and intensify the image thrown on to the stage, or elements of language which evoke our pleasure or our amusement. It is surely sensible to suppose that they were meant to do so. Watching this in play after play we can accustom ourselves to the way this dramatic artist built up his play; we can see the tricks at his command, and watch him using them over and over again. Even the simplest of these may be revealing. For example, the trick of making a character angry. Why is this so frequent? Does it allow psychological exploration? Not specially, since the cases are perfectly ordinary, and tell us nothing about angry people that we have not met hundreds of times in our own experience. Does it point any moral lesson, or rebuke any vice, as many people think comedy should do? Clearly not, since we laugh at the cases and do not take them to heart. Why seek for such 'clever' explanations, when the dramatic value of the trick is there, staring us in the face, as plain as all good dramatic effects should be? When Molière's fools get angry they reveal more than they would ever have said in cold blood. Determined to have any doctor for his son-in-law, Argan browbeats his daughter and gets annoyed with his servant when she mocks him by saying that he will not 'have the heart' to carry out his threats. By dint of contradicting her he is induced to admit that he is the opposite of a good father: 'Je ne suis pas bon, je suis méchant quand je veux.' The student may think that this is a point too simple to discuss, but it is for all that a point of dramatic technique, which clearly went down so well that its author repeats the whole section of dialogue in another play.

Is one not entitled to call this scientific study of drama? It does not start by asking questions which have been asked about other drama. It starts by examining the evidence, by trying to understand the terms in which problems are presented. It looks closely at the language, at the order of scenes and points, at any pattern which seems to emerge from that order. It aims in fact at watching so closely these puppets (for they are often no more than that) that we may see what was in the mind of their creator and manipulator.

Here is a field of investigation as yet largely unexplored. It may be called, properly in my view, the aesthetic of comedy. As I hope to show in this final chapter, it leads to conclusions which are at variance with much that has been assumed about Molière. This means that we must proceed cautiously, testing our findings. But we need not be worried about being led to new conclusions. The conclusions of tested evidence are a safer guide than any tradition.

Not all the tricks are as simple as that of inducing anger so that speech may betray the speaker. This is only one form of the very ancient dramatic technique of putting pressure on a character so that his reaction may shock or amuse the audience. To see the extent of Molière's fantasy one should study a famous scene, such as the second of *Le Misanthrope*. If we ask why he should have imagined this particular encounter, immediately after the exposition, the answer is not at once clear. A discussion of literary taste has not much to do with misanthropy. It may reflect a particular interest, either of the author and his friends, or of the audience. But this would involve the conclusion that the scene is episodic or auto-biographical, a conclusion which we should not accept until we are sure that the author had no principle of dramatic structure in mind: the episodes in *Le Misanthrope* may be as carefully planned as those in *Hamlet*. Those who read the comedy as a personal play may seek for Molière's own views of poetry, but this again implies that he was not concerned primarily with structure, and furthermore it assumes that we can gather from this scene what his views were. This is impossible. Did he prefer the *précieux* sonnet, which is obviously ridiculed? Or did he prefer the jingle about King Henry, which Alceste prefers? But Alceste is the fool of the play, and in this instance it is very likely that a Paris audience of 1666 would think his taste wrong-headed, like his other views.

Surely to any unprejudiced student of comic drama all these explanations seem far-fetched and improbable. There is clearly a structural, a properly dramatic, reason for the scene. It is excellent comedy to see a man of rigid principle confronted, immediately, with a test case, silly in itself, of a social butterfly offering eternal friendship and requesting advice on a sonnet. How or why Molière thought of the sonnet, whether Boileau or another friend suggested it, we may never know, and we do not need to know. Our business as students is to note how an actual test case has supplied so immediate an enrichment of the dramatic material. Everything about Oronte is absurd, so we have one fool facing another, i.e. something much more dramatic than the wrong view being confronted with the right view. The task of handling Oronte evokes all Alceste's natural politeness, a point which many beginners miss Alceste is much nicer than his principles: his courtesy makes him eat his words. Philinte has just dragged out of him that on principle he would say what he thinks, outright, even to a lady: 'Quoi, vous iriez dire a la vieille Émilie ...? ... Sans doute. — Vous vous moquez. — Je ne me moque point, Et je vais n'épargner personne sur ce point.' (81–88) But now, three times over, 'je ne dis pas cela'. This is good drama. And it becomes better still when he gets excited, and ceases to be polite: 'franchement...colifichets ... je me garderais de les montrer, etc.'

I have spent some time over what may seem very obvious, yet this elementary exegesis is not fashionable. The latest work[1] on *Le Misanthrope* bases its interpretation of the play on three factors: biography, psychology, morality. No wonder that such an analysis

---

[1] R. Jasinski, *Molière et le Misanthrope*, 1951, p. 324.

reaches conclusions which have almost nothing in common with severe stylistic discipline, with due consideration of dramatic structure, with a proper respect for the actual text. So then the way is open for rigorous study on new lines, for consideration of the text, in its proper context, and for exclusion of outside factors, which may or may not have had something to do with the text—in other words, for close attention to the artistic elements, in what is after all admitted by everybody to be first and foremost a work of art. This may seem obvious but it has hardly yet been carried beyond the elementary stage. And its implications are enormous.

One of these implications may shock a good many people, so perhaps it should be mentioned here. Briefly put, it amounts to saying that we should give 'psychology' a rest in explanations of Molière's work. In most of the textbooks it occupies a large place. The first thing to consider about a classical French play is, it would seem, the 'characters'. Molière's main characters are gravely discussed, and professors find it difficult to show that they are in any plain sense comic characters. Tartuffe, as a character, would be called sinister and Dom Juan cynical. This might well be so, if we were dealing with people in real life. And this is just what too many experts have assumed, that Molière offers a realist set of characters. But who said so? Who said that we must think of these famous rogues and fools as real people? It is an assumption, which has never been proved. The text indeed suggests something quite different. We know why the text was written: to provoke enjoyment by suggesting ridiculous ideas and postures. Is it not possible to do this without profound and accurate psychology? Some years ago the Abbé Bremond made a strong plea that Racine should not be thought of as primarily a psychologist but as a poet. Just as he found the actions and reactions of Racinian characters neither very new nor very subtle, so might it be claimed that in the case of Molière we have too easily assumed that the skill must lie in the accuracy of character-drawing. But poets need not be, and are not, accurate:

they are suggestive and imaginative. Perhaps the difficulty we con-
front here is that to speak of Molière as a poet is something new.
The professors do not so speak of him. Louis Jouvet, after much
experience of his work, both as reader and as actor, thought that
'poet' was the right description.

I am not here concerned to deny that Molière is a psychologist
or that he has portrayed human and mental reactions which may be
called subtle or penetrating. We may each of us have our own
opinion on such a point. In the interests of scientific study, I am
concerned to question the as yet unproven assumption that his
characters must be judged by their realism, as suggesting real
people. Much closer study of the plays is needed before anyone can
say with confidence whether that is the case or not. Meanwhile,
students should give serious thought to an alternative assumption
and see if it fits the facts any better: the assumption that Molière was
concerned to imagine cases of the ridiculous and the absurd, and
to present them in such a way as to please an audience. If we look
without bias at what he has presented, we shall (I think) be struck
by other features, such as energy, speed, change. To many of the
characters, as to their creator, a critic quoted earlier (p. 56) thinks
that the word 'quicksilver' should be applied. Modern French
acting supports this view: the plays are taken at speed; the illusion
is vivid rather than lasting. What scholars have found baffling as
a character 'in the round', suggesting a man of flesh and blood, is
much more easily understandable as a quick sketch, in which the
attitudes (and often the intellectual ideas suggested) are clearly the
main point. Again, the suggestion is that these are puppets, not
people. Once a point has been made, they can be put back in the
box. A case in point would be two scenes in *Dom Juan*, I. ii and
III. i, of which Jouvet and Jean Vilar have recently shown us afresh
the great dramatic power. Is it likely that master and man in 1664
would so talk, that the master would allow the valet to say what he
liked, to ask questions about belief and morality? Surely the reverse.

The audience enjoy hearing what they would never in actual life be able to hear. They are interested in the scandalous discussion far more than in either master or man.

I think that we may be touching here on what makes the charm of Molière's comedy: the gift of fantasy, of imagining a clash of ideas put forward by figures apparently very alive, but who fade or change as soon as the point is exhausted. To keep to the play we have in mind, characters like the poor man, or M. Dimanche, are alive in their scene, but have no depth or importance as people: they pop up, so to speak, and then disappear, not to be seen again.

If we study the actual evidence we shall find many things that puzzle us in this comedy. Let us welcome all these things as part of what Molière has created, as part of what he calls comedy. Here we come upon a big issue, not yet studied. In the ocean of bibliography devoted to Molière there is no single work which (to my knowledge) attempts a full investigation into this central question: what sort of comedy was it that Molière actually created and that has proved so powerful and successful as a form of art? This is not at all the same as the question: what were his ideas of what comedy should be? (to which I think there is no answer). Nor is it the question: into what types may we divide his comedies? The usual divisions into comedies of character, of manners, and farces really tell us nothing. No, the more I study him the more convinced I become that he was a poet of genius, who, almost without theories or moral intentions, succeeded in creating, time after time, dramatic situations which have proved living and suggestive, and which his own people consider to be comic. This creation, this suggestive power, this kind of poetry is the true centre of Molière study. To Anglo-Saxons it is new and strange even to speak of Molière as a poet, still more so to discuss his comedy. What we lack is not, I think, a sense of humour, but a valid philosophy of comedy. Only Meredith among leading English writers has attempted this. For most of us comic means funny, anything that may raise a laugh. This error is not confined to Anglo-Saxons. French scholars gravely discuss the comic element in Molière by asking how far it arouses laughter: '*Le Misanthrope* fait-il rire?'[1]

Of course, if comic and funny are not synonyms, then we can see why the books about Molière explain everything but the one thing that matters, the secret of his art. This error is so fundamental that we need not seek further reasons why Molière scholarship is so unsatisfactory. And personally I have little doubt that it is an error to equate comic and funny. There are plenty of laughs in Molière: there is plenty of wit and humour which may not make us laugh outright but as a contemporary said 'fait rire dans l'âme'. But all these should be seen, in my view, as outcroppings so to speak of the *vis comica*, not as the thing itself. In other words, the comedy is for ever emerging, erupting, into laughter, but that laughter is the comic shock coming to the surface, not to be equated with the thing itself. Let us go further into this basic point.

To begin with, what we call funny, what makes anybody laugh, is a concept restricted to the superficial. This we all admit when we say that something 'is no laughing matter'. Hazlitt thought Molière's greater plays hardly comic at all, because they did not make him laugh. For example, when Alceste describes his love to Célimène thus:

> Dans l'ardeur qu'il a de se montrer à tous
> Il va jusqu'à former des souhaits contre vous

this may not raise a laugh, unless the actor says it in an absurd tone, but it is a comic statement: it shows up the absurdity into which Alceste's mixture of doctrinaire principle and egoism may lead. The more he tries to rationalize his condition, the more contradictory and impossible it appears. What the poet here suggests is intellectually fascinating: we feel he has described the human condition upside down, for our enjoyment. We do enjoy it, and the

[1] Jasinski, op. cit., p. 293.

French naturally enjoy it more than we can, but we may well not laugh. It is certainly no laughing matter, for it goes deep and suggests profound things. It provokes what Meredith called 'the laughter of reason refreshed', which has little to do with what is just funny or amusing.

Perhaps Anglo-Saxons have not yet grasped what the French mean by *ridicule*, a major concept in seventeenth-century literature. If pressed to define it I would call it a combination of the real and the irrational. A thing is called *ridicule* that exists but which is at the same time a scandal to the intelligence. Not so much the wild fantasy of disordered or excessive imagination, but what happens, in defiance of prudence, reasonable calculation, logic, probability. Saint-Simon describes a riot at a royal funeral when the urn exploded, and calls it *ridicule*. The minute timing and placing, the various sets of people appointed to play a due and solemn part: the monks, the heralds, the ladies, the bearers, the ushers ... all these thrown into sudden disorder and panic by one unforeseen and incongruous little fact. The gap between the plan and the chaos is such that we laugh to read of it. They laughed too, as Saint-Simon is careful to note, but afterwards, when all was safe, free of infection, swept up. The happening was absurd, in itself; it became funny when it was seen to be harmless. This difference between comic and funny could be illustrated from Pascal, Retz, La Bruyère, but the most consistent theorist of *le ridicule* is the most natural and the least regarded, Molière himself. This is not demonstrably so, because the dramatist did not sign his work, but after M. Robert's rigorous analysis I think we may assume that Molière inspired, even if he did not actually write, the *Lettre sur l'Imposteur* of 1667. This pamphlet, in defence of a play which Molière was forced by public outcry to describe as an attack on vice, contains admirable descriptions and definitions of the comic. Molière defines it as the shape or perceptible outline of whatever is unreasonable: 'la forme extérieure et sensible que la providence de la nature a attachée à tout ce qui est déraisonnable'. He finds its essence to lie in *disconvenance* (incongruity) and in particular in whatever is a scandal to the intelligence: 'nous estimons ridicule ce qui manque extrêmement de raison . . . il s'ensuit que tout mensonge, déguisement, fourberie, dissimulation, toute apparence différente du fond, enfin toute contrariété entre actions qui procèdent du même principe, est essentiellement ridicule' (*G.E.* iv. 564).

When we read these passages let us remember that they come from over twenty years' experience of the stage and of French middle-class audiences. Do they not, more than any modern statement, enable us to understand what Molière actually created when he imagined for his public (and as it happened for posterity) pedants, fops, doctrinaires, a miser, an atheist, a hypochondriac? These 'ridiculous' figures are all placed in grotesque positions which to us suggest sanity and balance by showing up the contrary. We may laugh, but our enjoyment goes deeper than laughter, when reason meets fact: 'Hippocrate dira ce qu'il lui plaira, mais le cocher est mort' (see p. 112 above). Or where folly and cowardice are allied with delightful humanity, in Jourdain and Chrysale, and opposed to hard common sense or to domestic tyranny in Mme Jourdain and Philaminte. The fantasy escapes even from its original setting: Alceste is a fool, an 'atrabilaire', yet so eloquent that he seems at times to suggest the war of truth against everyday reality: the world is wrong and out of joint, no place for an honest man.

At times indeed in this new form of comedy the opposition of ideas is surprisingly suggestive and modern. What reader of *Dom Juan* has not felt on the Don's side at times against the attitude that will believe everything, that refuses to apply normal standards of evidence to interrogate authority, that swallows everything which assumes the expert's tone and jargon? A frequent form of this comic imagination is to portray experts as blinded outside the field of their expertise. The miser and the crook do not fail professionally, but in so far as they are blind to basic human facts like youth and sex. No drama suggests so well the comedy inherent in society, the comedy of the gospel character who sees the mote and misses the beam, the comic alliance of self-interest and entire lack of self-criticism.

In many ways Molière was probably not ahead of his time. It is absurd to think of him as nourishing a secret philosophy, as a prophet of secularism or even as sharing the views of Voltaire. The famous words in *Dom Juan*, 'Je te le donne pour l'amour de l'humanité', should not be wrenched out of their context. Yet the plays do show silhouettes of astonishing novelty and force. We might imagine their creator as a contemporary of Dryden, combining as he did, and perhaps in greater measure, lucidity and imagination. In the *Lettre sur l'Imposteur* we find this remark: 'Pour connaître le ridicule, il faut connaître la raison dont il signifie le défaut.' To write his scenes about unreason he must have possessed a singularly firm hold on reason, common sense, intellectual equilibrium. Perhaps my conclusion of 1949 (p. 134 above) was unjust to this intellectual serenity, which along with a powerful imagination has added a new dimension to comedy.

INDEXES

I. THE PLAYS

II. GENERAL

PRINTED IN GREAT BRITAIN
AT THE UNIVERSITY PRESS, OXFORD
BY VIVIAN RIDLER
PRINTER TO THE UNIVERSITY